Bernard LaFreniere, C.S.C.

Brother André

According to Witnesses

To Jeanne, my mother,
who knew Brother André
and spoke so highly about him.

Bibliothèque nationale du Québec.
National Library of Canada.
Legal Deposit – 4th quarter, 1997.
Second printing, 15 thousandth, 1997.
ISBN 2-920067-09-5

© ST. JOSEPH'S ORATORY
       3800 Queen Mary Road
       Montreal, QC
       Canada   H3V 1H6   Tel.: (514) 733-8211

Bernard LaFreniere, C.S.C.

Brother André
According to Witnesses

Seven Lectures
to the
Brothers of Holy Cross
in Austin, Texas

I wish to express deep appreciation to my friends and family, whose assistance and suggestions were most valuable.

I am particularly grateful to Blaine Burkey, a Capuchin friend, and to members of my Holy Cross family, William Dunn, Eveline Swaile and Michael McDonald, whose help was critical in bringing about this present edition.

I also thank Cecilia Lefebvre, a Holy Cross sister, who painted the oil portrait on the cover.

Blessed Brother André in 1912, at the age of 67.
Born on August 9, 1845, he died on January 6, 1937.

Contents

Foreword

With keen interest we admire the success of great artists, sports stars, scientists, and heads of state. Their achievements fire our imagination beyond our daily, limited horizons.

The saints play a similar role. They are not only our influential friends living with God; their lives and dreams can also inspire our own Christian commitment.

When Brother André died on January 6, 1937, all knew he was a saint. No one wanted his memory to be idealized, or changed, or forgotten in any way. So for eight years, an ecclesiastical tribunal called on 49 of the best witnesses and asked each a long series of questions. Their answers were taken in shorthand and transcribed so that they might reread and correct what they had said and then sign it under oath. A total of 3,335 pages of accurate, first-hand information were thus collected. Other Church officials were appointed by Rome in 1962 to conduct a similar process in Montreal, and 22 witnesses added another 900 pages on even more specific questions. Surely few individuals are better known now than the humble founder of Saint Joseph's Oratory.

The seven conferences which follow were prepared for the Brothers of Holy Cross in Austin, Texas. The story they tell is based on several biographies, but especially on the narratives of the witnesses, in their own words. Several of them spent much time with André and could enter, as it were, the intimacy of his heart and soul. They also provided a good insight into his religious community, the Congregation of Holy Cross.

May the reader enjoy his story as much as I enjoyed presenting it to his confreres in Texas.

Bernard LaFreniere, C.S.C.

Saint Joseph's Oratory in Montreal, Canada,
attracts more than 2,000,000 visitors annually.

Brother André with his friend and first biographer
Colonel George H. Ham in January, 1921.

The Miracle Man

Anyone who writes about Brother André today can easily feel like a fourth-generation interpreter, trying to explain different authors' analyses of what witnesses said more than 50 years ago.

Indeed several people who knew him wrote on his life and work on Mount Royal. The first was Father George A. Dion, who published a contemporary chronicle in the *Annals of Saint Joseph,* which he began at the Oratory in 1912.

George A. Dion, C.S.C.
1852-1918

This priest had been the general procurator of the Congregation of Holy Cross in Rome from 1892 to 1896, and for some time wrote in the *Annals of the Association of Saint Joseph,* a Holy Cross magazine founded in France in 1870 — the very year young Brother André entered the community.

Father Dion was also the provincial superior in Canada when the first Oratory was built. A tall man, he was quite impressive and serious and Brother André was a bit shy in his presence; but as the years went by, he became one of André's most dependable supporters.

Anticlerical laws passed in France in 1903 by Education and Cult Minister Émile Combes closed more than 2,000 Catholic schools and dispersed many religious communities. Most of the Holy Cross brothers and priests came to the United States and Canada. Their *Annals of the Association of Saint Joseph* were discontinued. After nine years, however, Father Dion decided to resume publishing them at Saint Joseph's Oratory with the first chronicle of the Shrine. Today this chronicle has become a basic source of information about Brother André and the beginning of his Oratory.

Two books on his life and work were published already in 1922. One was written by Colonel George H. Ham, a Protestant gentleman who served as publicity director for the Canadian Pacific Railway Company. The other was published in French and in English by Arthur Saint-Pierre, a sociology professor at the University of Montreal. A few years earlier, he had written a long article on the healing of Martin Hannon from Quebec City, a case that was much publicized in the newspapers in 1910.

A Catholic writer, William H. Gregory, wrote another small book "for the American pilgrims" a few years later. *Brother André of Saint Joseph's Oratory* was printed in New York in 1925.

These three books and the chronicle were the only works on Brother André when he died in 1937. Then Father Henri Paul Bergeron wrote his biography that became a best-seller in French as well as in English; 50 years later, *The Wonder Man* was still selling nearly 40,000 copies a year. Very few biographies published half a century ago can

muster the same interest, and Brother André has surely become one of the most popular Canadian citizens of his time.

We read these books now with pleasure. But we all know that a biography is somewhat like a tinted window or a grid between us and the person. Behind every phrase, there is a witness, someone who knew Brother André personally. Some were close friends who shared in his thoughts, his projects, his prayer, his dreams, his everyday joys and struggles, and all the events that took place.

With this in mind, we realize how wise the Church is in providing an opportunity for the witnesses to declare under oath, and then to correct and rewrite what they have said about a Servant of God. That is what makes a beatification process so important for future generations.

In the following pages, therefore, we will quote as much as possible from what the actual witnesses said in their own words.

Miracles

In Montreal, if you ask people, "Who was Brother André? What was so special about him?" The most common answer will be: "He performed miracles." When someone in

Canada says, "I cannot do that; I am not Brother André," it means, "I DON'T PERFORM MIRACLES."

So, the very name Brother André is associated with the notion of MIRACLES. No wonder Colonel Ham entitled his first biography: *"The Miracle Man of Montreal."*

The Miracle Man of Montreal

By
George H. Ham

Author of "Reminiscences of a Raconteur"

With a glowing tribute to the Miracle Man
by S. Morgan Powell.

When we read the thousands of pages of the acts of the beatification process, we are struck by the same fact — the notion of MIRACLES is everywhere. The witnesses answer every question to the best of their knowledge. But the longest answer, where it seems that they could speak on, and on, and on forever is question No. 50, the question about the MIRACLES. For instance, the first witness answered 49 questions in 20 pages, but he needed another 20 pages to answer question No. 50.

What Is a Miracle?

Now, before reading what they wrote, we could share a few thoughts on what a miracle is in theology and in the Christian tradition. It touches something very deep, maybe the most basic and the most original intuition of the existence of God. A miracle is intimately connected with faith.

The original text of the Gospel uses in Greek either "semeion" or "dynamis" for miracles. The former means a *sign* and the latter an act of *power*. Two English words, "dynamite", which means a *power* • ful explosive, and "semantics", the study of the *sign* • ification of terms, stem from the same two words. Miracles, therefore, refer to an act of POWER, a SIGN given by the Lord, and they may well be the most primitive intuition of the existence of God.

If you go to the Pacific Islands, in Polynesia for instance, you will find one word that seems to be at the root of every form of religious belief. The word is "Mana", and it refers to the idea of a supernatural power. Not only the concept but even the word is pretty much the same in several languages, not only in the Pacific Islands, but elsewhere in the world. Thus the Bible in Polynesian translates a "miracle" by "mana" — an act of Power.

The first Canadian aborigines were found in North America some 29,000 years ago. The Algonquins, in Montreal, also believed in a Supernatural Power whom they called "Manitou." Indeed, thousands of years before Christ, men and women were searching for God, and the living God manifested himself in SIGNS of his Power. His prophets Elijah and Elisha performed miracles in the ninth century B.C.[1] Miracles were also reported in the time of Jesus,

---

(1) See 1Kings 17 and 2Kings 2-5. Elijah worked a miracle on behalf of a widow who fed him in a time of famine; her meal jar and oil jug never ran dry. He raised her dead son to life. In the same way, his disciple Elisha raised a woman's son to life after praying to Yahweh. In Elisha's presence, a widow's oil cruet flowed until she had enough to repay her creditor. The prophet also healed the water in Jericho, multiplied the loaves and cured Naaman's leprosy.

throughout the history of the Church, and they are still found today.[1]

Two Common Mistakes

There are two common mistakes about miracles.

One is to try to possess, or to control the "Mana." Magicians have tried to do this in every culture, but the God of the Bible never submitted to magicians.

Notre Dame School in Cote-des-Neiges from 1869 to 1882.

Another mistake is to make a miracle a condition, or pre-requisite before faith. One says, "Unless I see a miracle, I will never believe." The Gospel says the opposite: "In that

---

(1) The Gospel reports 35 of Jesus' miracles, 17 of which are physical healings. Saint Peter and Saint Paul performed miracles, as well as many other saints after them: Saint Macarius in Egypt, Saint Brigid in Ireland, Saint Anthony of Padua in Italy, Saint Vincent Ferrer in Spain, Saint Martin of Tours in France, and so many others.

town, Jesus did not perform many miracles because of their lack of faith."[1] Indeed miracles are not the proof of faith, but it is faith that makes them possible, and they can be seen only through the eyes of faith. Brother André as a believer enabled them to happen according to the will of God.

With this in mind, let us now go back to his life story as told by the witnesses.

The First Miracles

Brother André in his early thirties.

It is difficult to tell exactly when the first healings took place. It seems they began early in his religious life. The first printed document dates back to when he was only 32, and in fact tells of events even earlier.

Brother Michel Giraudeau wrote to the *Annals of the Association of Saint Joseph,* the Holy Cross magazine published in France:

"On Sunday, March 31, 1878, I had someone drive me to Cote-des-Neiges" — a Montreal suburb, also known as Snowhill — "for the regular meeting of the Provincial

---

(1) Matthew 13:58. Also, "He could work no miracle there... He was amazed at their lack of faith." Mark 6:5-6.

Council. There, I asked little Brother André to fetch me some of the oil from the lamp of Saint Joseph, the oil about which he had told me marvelous things. The good Brother André did not believe he was authorized to give me what I was asking for, and I had to turn to Brother Ladislaus, who had greater authority, being the sacristan of Notre Dame School. That evening I applied a few drops from my precious vial on my wounded leg while invoking Saint Joseph, asking him to heal me and promising him, if I were healed, to go to communion the next day in thanksgiving. The following day, as I woke up, I felt no more pain; and after two days, only a scar remained. Since then, I resumed my regular work."

The author of this letter was among the first Holy Cross missionaries sent by Father Basil Moreau to Canada in 1847. The first group consisted of eight brothers, four sisters, and two priests,[1] most of whom were in their early twenties. Brother Michel was 19 years old and went back only once to France. Eventually he became one of the pillars of Holy Cross in Canada and one of André's most dependable friends. He died in 1900, four years before the building of the original chapel on Mount Royal.

Michel Giraudeau, C.S.C.

(1) Bishop Ignatius Bourget of Montreal asked for teaching brothers only, but Holy Cross sisters, brothers and priests worked together. A priest led the group; they helped one another and shared in the same budget. Among the newcomers, Brother Louis and Sister Clarisse Vermont were siblings, which made collaboration all the more natural.

Brother Michel was also a writer. That we know so many details about the life of the first sisters, brothers, and priests of Holy Cross in Canada is mostly due to his pen. In May of 1878, when he wrote to the publisher of the *Annals of the Association of Saint Joseph,* he was 50 and a provincial councillor. In the same letter, he went on telling about four other healings which had taken place earlier, when André was maybe 30 or 31 years old.

"I am not the only one who was healed with the oil of Saint Joseph. Last year, Brother Alexander had a more serious wound than mine. He had a fever, his whole leg was swollen and dark; the poor man could not stand on his feet and the doctors could do nothing. He began a novena during which he anointed his leg daily with Saint Joseph's oil. All of a sudden, he was relieved from his chronic pain."

A third case told by Brother Michel in his letter reads as follows:

"A servant in our house" — St. Laurent College, about three miles north of Mount Royal — "Mr. Joseph Bouthiller, was completely para-

St. Laurent College from 1862 to 1882.

lyzed by rheumatism in his arm. Brother André told him to rub his arm with some oil from the lamp of Saint Joseph.

Bouthiller followed the advice and that very same day was most astonished when he recovered the use of his arm."

Fourthly, "A good father of a family who had nothing but his daily work to earn a living for his family was losing his eyesight. His eyes were swollen, and he could not stand the daylight. The only medicine he used was some Saint Joseph's oil and, on the second day, he was cured and resumed his work, while blessing the adoptive Father of Jesus."

Still another healing was reported in Brother Michel's letter:

"Mrs. Grenier had diphtheria, a terrible disease that causes anguish, desolation and death among the families. She had lost all hope when she was given some Saint Joseph's oil. She anointed her throat, and her trust in the protector of Christian families paid off instantly. She was healed, and no one else in her house caught the disease."

Brother Michel ended his letter saying: "I will stop now. If I were to tell of all the wonders worked here by our good and powerful Saint Joseph, I would never end." That letter was dated May 9, 1878.

These five cases are most interesting since Brother André was still young. He had taken final vows only on February 2, 1874; and when the first healings took place, he still had 26 years to go before the first chapel would be built across the street from the school.

And as the miracles which first happened in 1877 during the early years of André's life as a Brother of Holy Cross continued until his death in 1937, they occurred for six decades.

In Holy Cross

All the while Brother André continued spreading devotion to Saint Joseph, whom Pope Pius IX had proclaimed the Protector of the Church on December 8, 1870, and whom the Congregation of Holy Cross had similarly honored since its beginning.

Father James Francis Dujarié founded the Brothers of Saint Joseph in 1820 to teach the boys in the aftermath of the French Revolution. In 1837 they merged with the Auxiliary Priests, a community founded two years earlier by Father Basil Anthony Moreau in the city of Le Mans, France. In 1841 Father Moreau added a society of

Father James F. Dujarié
1767-1838

sisters to his Congregation of "Holy Cross" — "Sainte Croix" being a suburb near the city of LeMans.

Father Moreau had dreamt of starting a place of pilgrimage to Saint Joseph at Charbonnière, the farm house near LeMans where he had established the novitiate of the Brothers. Even in Father James Dujarié's time, in the early 1820's, the devotion to Saint Joseph was well established among the Brothers.

In the chronicles we read that during Brother André's novitiate a flu epidemic had started to spread. The novice director — not Brother André this time — had installed a statue of Saint Joseph in plain view and had decided that the local community would make a novena to the Patron Saint of the Congregation. The epidemic stopped, the sick recovered and resumed their regular duties.

This is the kind of prayer Brother André found when he entered Holy Cross. Many other brothers and priests loved Saint Joseph and invoked him with the same confidence.

The early pupils of Notre Dame School, in Cote-des-Neiges, remembered how Brother André, while cutting their hair or in conversations with them, spoke often about the earthly father of Jesus. He told them to invoke Saint Joseph and to have confidence in him. The youngsters loved Brother André especially in his early years, when he was closer to them. Although he was a simple man, he was friendly, lively and quick-minded. So they related well with him, and many remained good friends for life.

Miraculous Cures

Once, apparently when André was still a young brother, a youngster had a bad fever and the doctor told him to stay in bed in the infirmary. Brother André went to see him and

A class of Notre Dame School in 1903.

said: "You're not sick, you little lazy bones! Go and play with the others!" The boy did not wait to be told a second time. He jumped out of bed, dressed, and went to play. The superior and the doctor were amazed, and although Brother André explained that Saint Joseph had cured the boy, they told him not to do this any more. But the word spread that, in fact, the boy WAS very sick and that Brother André had HEALED him with his confident prayer to Saint Joseph.

This is very much in the manner of Brother André: "Get up, little lazy bones! Go and play with the others! You're not sick any more!" Such phrases were terms of affection among our old folks!

Community tradition also tells how in 1884, when Brother André was 39, a woman suffering from rheumatism came to see him. He was busy scrubbing the floor, and when someone told him why she had come, he answered simply, "Let her walk!" and went on scrubbing the floor. But people insisted; so Brother André looked at the woman and said, "You're not sick any more. You may go back home." And the woman was healed.

According to the witnesses, 1884 was also the time when growing numbers of sick people started visiting the school regularly; so for at least 53 years Brother André lived with a reputation for healing.

Let us now go back to what the witnesses said in the beatification process in the early 1940's.

In the Words of the Witnesses

One said, "I witnessed one of Brother André's miracles. A man was brought to the Oratory, and he was tied up to a stretcher. Brother André came out of his office, looked at him, and said to those who had brought him up the hill, 'Untie him and let him walk.' Then, without even waiting to see the outcome, he entered the residence for his noon meal. Indeed, the man was healed, which caused quite a sensation. But Brother André had gone his way and was probably eating lunch with the rest of the community."

This story shows the humility of André and how he never tried to attract attention to himself. Yet, he himself said, "A healing is good, not only for the person who is healed, but for all those who hear about it."

Another witness said, "One day a man came to see Brother André and said to him, 'When I invoke Saint Joseph, I never get anything. But when I ask you, then I get what I want.' Brother André was so upset that he started trembling and quivering, and he showed the man to the door." To him, what the man said was almost a blasphemy, as though a miracle could be effected by human power.

Indeed this is an all-important feature of Brother André. He got angry for only one reason — when people said HE had a power to heal them. The fact that the favors came from God, through Saint Joseph, and not from him, was the most important point in his life. And he always put his full energy into defending that.

In the process for beatification, the Devil's Advocate asked us if that was not a lack of fortitude, a show of anger, and therefore of weakness. In the answer, we compared this anger with the scene when Jesus cast the merchants out of the Temple, in the second chapter of Saint John: "Jesus made a whip out of some cord, he drove them all out of the Temple, cattle and sheep as well, scattered the money-changers' coins, knocked their tables over..." and so on. Jesus was not only meek, he was strong in holding to essential points. One may find another example in the 23rd chapter of Saint Matthew, when he called the scribes and Pharisees hypocrites seven times in a row. Jesus was addressing the religious leaders of his time and his language was at least as strong as that of Brother André when he showed to the door the man who claimed that miracles came from him and not from God!

In 1910, at the age of 65.

Another witness was there the day that the chaplain to the King of England came to see him. The chaplain wanted to be nice and told him that the King himself had heard about his work and that he sent him his greetings. Brother André listened to all that reverently for two or three minutes, and then he said, "You will excuse me; many sick people are here today!" He had not at all been impressed.

Here is another fact as told by one of the witnesses:

"Mr. Sénécal was in his thirties, and he worked for the railway company. He had injured his leg and went to see Brother André one year after the accident. He paid several visits, but to no avail. Meanwhile his wound extended from his foot up to his knee, and surgeons decided to amputate his leg, because the bone itself had turned black from the ankle to the knee, and they couldn't do anything. Sénécal decided to wait until his novena was completed. Then he went to the hospital twice for the amputation. But since there was no room for him in the hospital, he went back home and the amputation was again postponed. Brother André then advised him that he should come and make a novena with him in his room over the original chapel. He remembered that the stench of the wound was awful, and it was late in the fall and too cold to open up the windows.

"One night Brother André was invoking Saint Joseph, and he prayed through the Precious Blood of Our Lord, asking that Sénécal might be healed. And all of a sudden the man felt that he was. He stood up, and as soon as the prayer was finished, started jumping up and down with joy. On the next day," the witness said, "a regular driver of Brother André drove the man to the hospital, so that the doctors might witness the healing. But none of them wanted to recognize Sénécal in spite of all his identity papers. They said it was absolutely impossible that such a serious wound would be healed so perfectly in so little time."

Another witness told this case:

"Mrs. Forest, from Joliette" — a small town 60 miles north of Montreal — "had a paralyzed arm following the birth of a child. She could not move her arm, so I drove her to see Brother André and asked him to rub the woman's arm with a medal of Saint Joseph. He did not want to do it; instead, he asked me to rub her arm with a Saint Joseph's medal." — The fact here is that, many years before, he had rubbed the arm of a little girl, and someone had reported the case to the superior, who had told Brother André never to touch females, even on the forearm, for fear that people would accuse him of being immodest. He never did it afterwards. — "So," the witness said, "I rubbed the woman's forearm and kept looking at Brother André, in order to join him in his prayer. All of a sudden, her arm became flexible again; she was healed. That was in the first years of the original chapel."

Father Clement, the first priest to serve at Saint Joseph's Oratory, told of still another case:

Adolphe Clement, C.S.C.
1874-1940

"A man was crippled after his two feet had been crushed so badly that only the skin, as it were, kept them together. Before they brought him to the Oratory, the men made two wooden boxes so as to protect his feet. When Brother André saw him, he started rubbing the wooden boxes. When I saw him doing this I said, 'What are you doing, Brother André? Do you really believe that, by rubbing these wooden boxes, you will make his feet grow?' But Brother André did not answer. He did it his own way then, and again on the next day, and on the third, and on the fourth day. Then he said to his patient, 'Now, let us remove these boxes, I believe your feet are doing quite well.' So they removed the boxes. Indeed his feet were healed."

This case is particularly interesting, because Father Clement was a somewhat nervous and authoritarian man. Brother André was simple, a poor Canadian peasant from the 19th century. But he was well adapted to the people. Father Clement thought he knew better and reacted to such a naive situation. However, he respected the ways of André, who once again proved to be right.

His Sense of Humor

Another feature of Brother André as a person was his keen sense of humor. Although he had very little schooling, he was bright, keen, and quick-minded, especially in grasping funny situations.

April 19, 1927.

One day he saw a woman picking some little green apples at the bottom of the hill. When she finally entered his office, she asked to be relieved from a stomach pain. Brother André could not help saying, "Why don't you eat some little green apples?" The woman blushed and had to admit her petty theft.

The sick who came to see him were not always so quick-minded. Here is another example told by witness Joseph Oliver Pichette:

"One morning, when I was with Brother André in his office, a young man came and his leg was sore. He said to Brother André, 'I've been coming to the Oratory for a year and am ending another novena today. If I'm not healed,

I'll have my leg amputated!' 'Do you want me to call the surgeon?' Brother André asked, and then he said, 'What results did you get out of visiting your doctors?' The man didn't answer and so Brother André made a deal: 'Well, listen. You begin one more novena today, and if your leg doesn't get better, I'll cut it off myself.' But the man got very angry and left the office.

"So I went to talk to him," the witness said, "and I explained that in fact, Brother André had almost promised him that he would be healed. I told him to go back and to apologize to Brother André: 'Go tell him you'll make the novena as he asked.' Brother André repeated the same words as above. The man made the novena and was healed."

The same witness told another similar story:

"Emile Laporte was 26 years old. He worked as a presser in a clothing factory. His feet were so swollen that the doctor told him he was very ill and eventually could die of this illness. So I drove him to see Brother André. The latter talked with him gently for a while. Then he looked at him and said, 'What movement do you have to perform on the pressing machine?' Then the man started pulling his leg up and down, and up and down, and up and down. I found that funny and said to Brother André, 'Well, obviously he CAN do his work.' 'Surely,' Brother André said with a big smile. 'You come back tomorrow.' The man did come back, and he was healed. Brother André was 85 years old at the time."

The Non-Catholics

It was said many times that Brother André practiced ecumenism out of his own common sense at a time when even the word was not well known. Several witnesses pointed out that people around him were surprised that he took so much time welcoming Protestants, Jews, Masons, and others, who at the time,

Brother André in 1920.

were often considered enemies of the Catholic Church. In fact, he not only welcomed them, but visited them in their homes. With his good, sound judgment, he could cross barriers and touch people's hearts, and many of these people were healed.

Here is one such story, again in the words of a witness:

"Brother André told me that, as he was coming back from New England, a priest told him he should go and visit an old man who was sick. In fact, the old man was a Mason. So Brother André showed him a medal of Saint Joseph and explained that many people had been healed by Saint Joseph after rubbing themselves with this medal. The old man agreed and Brother André started rubbing him with the medal. Finally the man was healed."

Many cures were not instantaneous. Sometimes Brother André had to insist before people were renewed in faith and then healed. Here is another case involving a Mason:

"One evening I drove with Brother André to the house of a Mr. Lefebvre. He had told me that the man was paralyzed. Brother André entered the room while I stayed with Mrs. Lefebvre. She told me that her husband was a Mason and that he hated all priests and brothers. But he could not talk, due to his paralysis. We could hear Brother André; he tried to help him say the names of Jesus, Mary, and Joseph. But the man would not repeat the names. On the way home, I told Brother André what his wife had told me, that he was a Mason. Brother André did not answer. But he said, 'This man will never speak unless he says the names of Jesus, Mary and Joseph.'

"In fact, the man resisted and he remained paralyzed for two more years. The pastor of the parish went to see him frequently, but to no avail. One day he said, 'It's really too bad! You will die without the sacraments; and after you die, your body will not even be brought into a church.' On the next day, the man finally asked for a piece of paper and he wrote that he wanted to see the priest. As soon as he began his confession, he recovered his speech. He lived several years after he was healed."

The least we can say is that this man was hard to heal!

André suffered from stomach pain. When it became more acute, he tended to be short-tempered. Here is one such case in the words of witness Joseph Pichette:

"A Protestant lady came to see Brother André and I was with him in his office. She kept talking, and talking, and talking so much that Brother André could not even say a word. He finally looked at her and said, 'If you don't want to listen to me, then you don't need me. So why don't you just go away.' He rang his little bell so that someone else entered. Then Brother André had tears in his eyes and said to me, 'If this woman can forgive me what I just did, she will be healed.' About 10 minutes later she came back to thank Brother André. She was healed."

The interior of the original chapel in 1909.

Here is another case which happened while Brother André was visiting his family in Woonsocket, Rhode Island. This story was also told by Joseph Pichette, the first witness in the beatification process.

"A man had been undergoing treatments for a long time with a physician. He suffered from bone tuberculosis, and his backbone was in very poor shape. He suffered a lot. When people heard that Brother André was in town, they said they would drive him to the Miracle Man whenever he wished to see him. But the man said he did not believe much in all that stuff and that he had no confidence in healings.

But his wife insisted, and he finally agreed that one of his friends would drive him to see Brother André.

"Actually, the man could walk only with crutches and very painfully. He also had to wear a plaster orthopedic corset. After talking to him, Brother André said, 'Give me your crutches and start walking.' But instead, the man hesitated. So Brother André himself took his crutches away from him. Then the man walked and asked Brother André if he would not also remove his plaster corset. The latter answered that he was going to go to his house on the following day, and that he would see to it. The next day, he asked, 'Could you come to Montreal during the summer?' The man said he would.

"Meanwhile, the doctor had told the man's wife that her husband was soon going to die of his illness. However, the man went to Montreal and saw Brother André again. He was in pain and completely bent over. But Brother André

A general view of Saint Joseph's Oratory in 1912.

removed his plaster corset. The man had also a wound on his back, due to his bone tuberculosis.

"While in Montreal, the man visited the Oratory each day for two or three weeks. Brother André during that time used some Saint Joseph's oil and rubbed his back. Finally the man was healed. His spine straightened up; he could stand straight again and walk normally.

"From then on, this man was perfectly healed and traveled every year to the Oratory to thank Saint Joseph and Brother André. The latter also visited him every time he went to see his family in Rhode Island."

As in the Time of Jesus

On certain days, several cures took place and we may well imagine that the atmosphere on Mount Royal must have been somewhat like that in Capernaum in the time of Jesus. People even forgot to say "Thank you." A witness told the following two stories:

"About 1911, on a Sunday afternoon, a young man came walking on two crutches. Both his legs dragged as he took each step. Brother André talked to him and then said, 'Give me your crutches and walk!' The man obeyed. Finding himself on his legs, he became so nervous and excited that he did not even say 'Thank you.' He ran down the steps to the street and took the trolley car back home without a word, while people looked at him through the window."

Only a half hour later, a man came and told Brother André that his arm was paralyzed, that he could no longer use it. André told him to put his hat on his head. The man tried once, and then a second time, and then a third time.

"Brother André told him, 'Make a novena. You will begin by going to confession and to communion.' But the man answered, 'It's been 25 years since I stopped going to confession.' 'You may come and sleep in my room tonight', Brother André answered, 'I'll find a priest for you.' And the man did come back. He went to confession and to communion on the next day." His paralysis disappeared.

During the beatification process of Brother André, a total of 125 cases of healings were told by the witnesses. These are only a few examples.

The interior of the original chapel in 1910.

Detail of the altar in 1910.

Saint Joseph's Oratory in September, 1910.

How Did the Oratory Begin?

If we were to trace the beginning of Saint Joseph's Oratory in Montreal, we would probably have to go back a long time before the actual opening of the first chapel in 1904; perhaps to the end of the 1800's, when lonely pilgrims were praying on the hilltop before a painted statue of Saint Joseph which Brother André had placed under a small wooden shelter there; or perhaps even ten or fifteen years earlier, when many visitors prayed with André near the entrance of Notre Dame School in Cote-des-Neiges. Saint Joseph's Oratory was already there in the people's prayer.

In His Family

In fact, if we want to find the real beginning of the Oratory, which literally means a place for prayer, it would be best to go way back into the youth of Alfred Bessette, the young boy who was later to be known as Brother André.

His parents married in a small town, some 30 miles southeast of Montreal, and the young couple looked somewhat like the one in Nazareth. Isaac Bessette and Clothilde Foisy were poor; Isaac was registered as a carpenter and his bride, a native of Saint Joseph's Parish in Chambly, was only seventeen years old. Therefore, from an early age, Alfred Bessette knew the earthly father of Jesus almost as a member of his own family, and certainly as a very close

Isaac and Clothilde married in Saint Matthias Church.

and approachable friend. Later in life, he would say in confidence to one of his friends, "I've always had this great devotion to Saint Joseph, and it came from my mother."

The foundations of his work were there well before the construction of the stone monument. Most of it was in Alfred's family prayer. Years later, it would turn into a popular movement, then a chapel, and then a stone monument which grew around the people's prayer.

It is a well-known fact that Alfred Bessette loved to pray during his childhood. It is also known that the provincial council hesitated some time before accepting him as a member of Holy Cross because of his poor health. It was feared that he would soon become a burden for the community. His novice director had to intervene by saying, "Even if this young man becomes unable to work, he will still be very much able to pray." And his word tipped the scale: André stayed with Holy Cross. Indeed, he prayed a great deal and he invited others to pray with him with all the faith, perseverance, and steadfastness requested by the Gospel.

A new Notre Dame School was built in 1882.

Spontaneous Publicity

Brother André was a simple man. At Notre Dame School, the pupils' parents found him easy to deal with, and they loved his deep faith, his friendliness, his unpretentious common sense. They started talking to him about their personal problems, their illnesses, and even about their failings. André promised to pray with them and all knew how much he did. The healings which followed were decisive in the further developments of his work.

It is often said that good makes no noise. But if that good is out of the ordinary, then the news spreads. All too soon, it happened with Brother André. His clients grew so numerous that the school was invaded.

There was no wooden chapel, no crypt and no basilica; however, one could tell that Saint Joseph's Oratory existed more and more in the doorkeeper's cell of Notre Dame College in Cote-des-Neiges. Meanwhile the disabled, the poor, the sick and the lame entered the school.

The doorkeeper's cell.

And that created problems. Some of the parents wondered, "Some of these sick people may be contagiously ill and should not enter our children's school as they do. What do the superior, and the doctor, and the other brothers think about this?"

A Cumbersome Movement

Secretly the superior disapproved, and Doctor Joseph A. Charette even more so. The latter, in fact, was a most influential member of the parish and did not hide his feelings: "Brother André is a quack and should stop that nonsense immediately." So he started telling anyone who wanted to listen to him, "This doorkeeper knows nothing about medicine; he should definitely stop caring for the sick."

A group of pupils of Notre Dame School in 1888.

The student director agreed: "He is covering the patients with oil. That's not prayer; that's superstition!" He too openly laughed at Brother André. Several of his confreres shared his opinion.

Before the situation got out of hand, the superior intervened and decided that Brother André was to stop welcoming the sick. The latter agreed with his superior, as always. But the people did not see it that way, and since he was the doorkeeper, he had to welcome everybody. The more people heard about the marvelous deeds performed by

Saint Joseph because of André's prayer, the more they came and showed up at all hours of the day. For some time, they would remain outside the school, on the grounds, since the doorkeeper had been ordered not to welcome them any longer.

The superior's solution soon became pointless. People insisted so much he had to let André welcome them after the parlor was closed. Then they obtained permission to wait for

him in a small trolley station across the street from Notre Dame School. The solution lasted a few years. But as the prayer movement continued to grow, those who did not know about the new regulations still turned up at the door.

At Last: A Chapel

A final decision remained possible: it was to steer all this movement towards the mountain. It so happened that

Notre Dame School had just purchased a piece of land on the hillside, across the street.

For a long time now, Brother André had wanted to build a chapel, an oratory dedicated to Saint Joseph. He spoke about it on several occasions, but without results. One of his best friends, Jules Maucotel, a town clerk, went to see the superior with him, but to no avail.

Stage By Stage

One day Brother André was sick. That was not unusual, but this time the local superior was sick with him in the same room. That gave him the time to talk about his project of a chapel, and he obtained permission to take a small statue to the hilltop. It was a plaster statue of Saint Joseph, donated by a friend, and painted by a confrere. He put it under a small wooden shelter, on the hilltop. Then accompanied by a student or a friend, he often went up to pray before the statue.

He then obtained permission to keep, for his dreamed of Oratory, the offerings brought by people who had been healed as well as the nickels he collected from the students when he cut their hair. He thus saved $200, a sum considered sufficient to initiate the project.

Thomas Prefontaine, the father of one of the pupils, donated all the wood. Brother Abundius Piché, the school's carpenter, did the work while André collected the funds. The superior had told him, "Go and tell Saint Joseph that there will be a chapel ONLY if you can find the money."

Lay Friends

Fortunately ever since the beginning of the project, Brother André was not alone. A group of lay people surrounded him with their enthusiasm and support. They were a printer's employees, a house builder, an administrator, two lawyers, and a medical doctor. In addition to bringing in their personal contributions, these friends of Brother André became zealous promoters of the project.

The original chapel in 1904.

Even Saint Joseph seemed to get personally involved. One day there came a stone mason who lived near the school, a giant of a man, who was suffering from a stomach tumor. He was no longer able to digest his food and grew thinner and thinner each day. So he came to see Brother André.

Abundius Piché, C.S.C.

The latter had only one thing in mind: "If Saint Joseph heals you, will you come and work with me on the mountain?" The mason agreed, but without believing much in Brother André's words. However, the next morning at a quarter of six, the mason came and ate breakfast with him. Then, he immediately set to work — he was cured! The fact only added to the enthusiasm of André's friends.

The undertaking was not so simple as it seemed. A gazebo already erected on the hill had to be torn down. The ground was excavated, stones were removed, some of the trees were cut down, and a plateau was leveled to make room for the chapel. Finally, an access road was opened to the plateau.

Several times Brother André had to tell his employees, "Next week I'll have no more money to pay you, and I have no permission to run into debt." But invariably, on the next Monday, the work resumed; a few generous benefactors had renewed their support.

The first Mass in the original chapel on October 19, 1904.

The chapel, completed by mid-October, was so small it could scarcely hold the altar, the priest and a few altar boys. Two large doors opened at the rear onto the grass, where two rows of benches had been set up.

The blessing of the chapel was held on a Wednesday, October 19, 1904. The vicar-general of the diocese presided over the ceremony, which was attended by the pupils of the school, their teachers, and friends of Brother André. Some journalists were also present and published a report the following day.

Under Rain and Sun

The little chapel looked pretty under the foliage, and certain celebrations were already drawing rather large crowds. But the heat in the summer, then the wind, the cold, and the rain more often than not prevented the pilgrims from praying in comfort.

One event was especially memorable. On the feast of Our Lady of the Snows, Sunday, August 5, 1906, the whole parish had gathered around the Oratory. The celebration was proceeding smoothly, but during the sermon given by a Franciscan Father, a heavy downpour fell on the audience. Everybody ran down the hill, but they all got soaked. The archivist wrote that evening: "The celebrant

ended the Holy Sacrifice as a low Mass." Everyone was disappointed.

No doubt Brother André's friends insisted they should get permission to built a shelter behind the chapel so as to avoid the same situation in the future. In fact, André was authorized to go and see the Archbishop of Montreal and ask him for permission to enlarge the chapel and heat it during the winter. But he did not succeed.

Archbishop Paul Bruchési.

The superior wrote in his personal diary: "The providential moment has not yet come, since His Grace postponed the study of this question."

The Stream of Visitors

Meanwhile, at Notre Dame School, the endless stream of visitors continued to swell. The sick and the afflicted came directly to the school door, where they were told that Brother André was not allowed to welcome them there. They had to cross the road again and wait for him in the trolley station.

The trolley passengers, however, complained about the presence of so many sick people in their station. One of them reported the case to the Montreal Board of Public Health. A doctor sent by the City to investigate the matter questioned Brother André, who explained how he cured with prayer, faith, and a bit of Saint Joseph's oil. "If it is so," the doctor summed up, "you have nothing to worry about." The report he submitted was in every way favorable to André.

Further Progress

His friends, however, were still not satisfied. The chapel was definitely too small; it had to be enlarged and heated in the winter. In order to give more weight to their interventions, they formed an association and held meetings in their homes.

On June 5, 1908, they persuaded the provincial superior himself to preside over one of their meetings during which it was decided: "That we shall erect two rows of ten-inch-square wooden posts, from the Oratory to the rock of the mountain, which will give a length of 100 feet and a width of 40 feet, with a roof covered with tar paper."

The shelter was completed on July 1, and its inauguration took place a month later. Six hundred pilgrims had gathered for the occasion and the majority found a shelter from the sun.

Early in September, however, the cold wind began to blow under the shelter and the pilgrims could no longer pray as they wanted. The committee met once more, this time in the absence of the superior, in the residence of Contractor Alfred Rousseau. It was on a Wednesday, September 9, 1908. They decided that they themselves would take charge of the project. One week later, they presented the provincial superior with a petition bearing 2,000 signatures, and requesting that the Oratory be enlarged and heated in the winter. They would take charge of financing the project.

Work began the following week and lasted two months. The two large doors at the entrance of the chapel were removed. On either side, four of the posts of the new shelter were surrounded with walls. At the rear, a four-section folding door opened on the rest of the shelter. A part of the new shelter thus formed the nave of the new Oratory, and the primitive chapel became its sanctuary. The building was solid, had storm windows, and a coal-burning stove gave enough heat for the pilgrims. Its inauguration took place on November 22, and 200 people attended.

Saint Joseph's Oratory in December, 1908.

The First Winter

At the end of 1908, more and more of André's clients made their way directly to the chapel. Several times a week someone else had to take his place as the school's door-keeper, to give him more time to devote to the pilgrims.

In the winter, however, it became difficult to climb the mountain. Stairs were needed all the way up the icy slope. It was also felt that an office should be built near the chapel, where the sick could talk to Brother André without disturbing those who had come to pray in silence.

 Then the committee decided to build a house consisting of a souvenir shop, a restaurant, an office for Brother André, and a waiting room. Again, they obtained permission from the superior and did everything themselves at their own expense. The manager, a nephew of the bursar, Father Renaud, was allowed to run the store and restaurant for a reasonable length of time then so as to compensate for his expenditures.

The same year, a long wooden sidewalk was built between the road and the top of the hill. Pilgrims could now go up the 140 steps as they liked, even in winter.

Saint Joseph's Oratory of Mount Royal had all it needed to welcome the pilgrims. They were not long in coming, and their number grew so that, during the summer, the provincial superior had to relieve Brother André entirely from his duty as doorkeeper of Notre Dame School. He officially appointed him GUARDIAN OF THE ORATORY.

Therefore, he put together the few things he had and settled into the small room built by Father Renaud's nephew. The store clerk installed himself much the same way in another room.

General view in 1909.

A Decisive Stage

The year 1909 had marked a turning point in Brother André's work. Only five years earlier, the chapel was seen as a solution to the problem of having too many undesirable visitors in the school. Now Saint Joseph's Oratory had an existence of its own. More and more, it enjoyed the support of superiors and was making some definite progress, especially since Brother André was living on the premises.

It is noteworthy that thus far, almost everything was done by lay friends of André, with the help of Brother Abundius Piché, the school carpenter. The Oratory had not been called for by a superiors' chapter or by a council meeting, but by a committee of lay people who insisted on and obtained every permission before every move. Behind them was the crowd of sick and afflicted who had, as it were, broken open the doors of Notre Dame School in order to gain access to Brother André's prayer. Right from the beginning, the Oratory was a vast popular movement and, one may well say, THE WORK OF SAINT JOSEPH.

A few statistics from that period reveal pretty well what was happening. On June 6, 1909, the blessing of the first bell took place. We still have it in the museum; it weighs 1,024 pounds. A crowd of 3,000 persons gathered for the ceremony. On August 22 of the same year, a statue of Mary

A gathering of people near the original chapel about 1910.

was blessed; 2,000 people attended. During the summer, the committee of laymen published the first prayer book for use at the Oratory; 5,000 copies were sold out in one year. That year alone, more than 29,500 letters were received. More than 80 letters arrived per day; and since Brother André could hardly read or write, a secretary had to be appointed to answer all these letters.

The Project of a Whole Population

The popular movement surrounding Saint Joseph's Oratory had now become irreversible. Brother André spent long hours in prayer and led the people along the Stations of the Cross, his favorite devotion. The pilgrims attended Mass, received Holy Communion, and still called upon priests for the sacrament of forgiveness. For hundreds of people, the new chapel had become a place of prayer, a contact point between their everyday lives and their personal relationship with God.

Brother André was first and foremost, like all great religious personalities throughout the history of the Church, a MAN OF PRAYER, a person with an explicit relationship with God. He prayed each day of his life, several times a day.

February 2, 1925.

He prayed alone, in his room, while traveling, in the chapel, with the sick, and in large gatherings.

The Gospel shows how the Apostles had been attracted and fascinated by the prayer of Jesus. Something similar was happening with André's prayer. People felt that it was real and they wanted to pray like him. Some of his friends used to say, "Here is a man who works all the time and prays constantly." And again, "He spends all his time talking about God to people and about people to God." His faith was lived in a daily service and expressed in a daily prayer.

Signs From God

André's prayer was matched by a growing number of remarkable favors. People spoke more and more spontaneously of "miracles." In 1916 alone, 435 cases of cures were reported, which amounted to more than one cure per day, not including those not reported.

Brother's attitude towards the cures was well known: they all came from God, and through the personal care and prayer of Saint Joseph. He quickly corrected those who asked him to heal them or who credited him with a miracle, as though a miracle could come from our own human power. Yet, he wanted all the cures to be known and he himself, with his friends, displayed the crutches and other devices of those who had been healed.

About 1906, the provincial superior visited the chapel and noticed this "trophy of crutches" on the right side of the altar. He said, "Come on, Brother André, we are not going to begin this kind of thing here. Please remove all these crutches." André, who always was remarkably obedient, removed them. Some time later, however, he was sick in the infirmary as was often the case. The provincial superior was sick in the same room. André talked to him about different things, and then said to him, "You know, Father, the crutches were put into the chapel only when the cure had

lasted for a few weeks." Then he went on to say, "You always explain that miracles are SIGNS given by God. Well, if the Lord gives us signs, it should not be for us to hide them!"

The provincial superior gave it a second thought and, after a while, gave permission to André and his friends to put the crutches back where they belonged, into the chapel.

A "trophy" in Brother André's time.

To many of his friends, he explained, "These cures do much good not only to the person who is healed, but also to all those who hear about them."

One priest who lived with him at the Oratory for nine years, Father Emile Deguire, asked him, "Can you tell me how you know the difference between a person who is going to be healed and one who will not be. To one you say, 'Make a novena, rub yourself with the medal and the oil of Saint Joseph, pray with confidence...' and to someone else you only say, 'Stand up and walk!' How can you tell that one is going to be healed?"

Brother André answered very simply, "Sometimes, it is obvious...." What more could he say? As it seems, he received directly from the Lord the intuition that a sign was going to oc-
cur under the eyes of the witnesses.

Some cures were remarkable, such as the case of Martin Hannon, an Irishman from Quebec

Father Emile Deguire, C.S.C., in 1974.

City. He was a foreman with the Canadian Pacific Railway Company and attended the unloading of large marble blocks. While he was looking elsewhere, one of these blocks toppled over behind him and fell on his feet and legs in such a way that the bones were crushed to small pieces. That was in October of 1908.

With the surgery of the time, after one year of operations and treatments of all kinds, Martin Hannon barely managed to drag himself painfully about on two crutches. He then heard about Brother André and his developing Oratory on the hillside of Mount Royal.

This case was carefully documented by Arthur Saint-Pierre, one of André's first biographers, who wrote:

"On January 9, 1910, Martin Hannon took the train and arrived at the Oratory in the company of a friend, Joseph Lacroix, who helped him go up to Brother André's office. There, at the single touch of Brother André's hand, Hannon's legs were instantly cured. He left his crutches at the Oratory and walked back unassisted. The newspapers of the day, and in particular 'La Patrie' of January 10, 1910, widely publicized the cure. The seriousness of the accident had been attested to by the patient, the members of his family, his fellow workers, and the chief surgeon of Hotel Dieu Hospital in Quebec City."

Such incidents could only attract more crowds even in the middle of winter. In February, 1910, the superior wrote in his chronicle: "Life is in full swing on the mountain as in the finest days of summer."

New Developments

The nave of the chapel, which then measured 30 feet in length by 40 feet in width, had become too small. It had to be extended under the shelter of 1908, before the feast of Saint Joseph. On March 18, the new annex, similar in every respect to the first, was opened to pilgrims.

The work of the painters inside the chapel had just been completed, and now the Oratory promoters wanted a sacristy topped by a small room and a bell-tower. For the first time, plans were drawn by a professional architect, Dalbe Viau. This part of the chapel is still in existence today.

The increasing number of pilgrims called upon priests at all hours of the day. In the summer of 1910, Father Adolphe Clément was appointed to the Oratory. He was almost blind upon his arrival and told Brother André about his anxieties. Brother André simply said, "Tomorrow, you shall read your breviary." The next day, Father Clément had regained his eyesight. Specialists, after examining his eyes, told him:

"But you are blind, Father!" Much to their amazement, Father Clément could see.

But one priest, even though he could see, was not sufficient. What was needed was a residence with an entire community. A contract was signed for the construction of a three-story brick residence. The foundations were laid in October of 1910.

Brother André, Fathers George Dion and Adolphe Clement in 1910.

On weekdays that year, the Oratory received, on the average, between 400 and 500 people a day. For large gatherings, the chapel soon became much too small. Obviously, some more spacious and permanent buildings should be considered.

After lengthy studies and discussions, on March 19, 1914, less than ten years after the building of the first chapel, a contract was signed with architects Dalbe Viau and Alphonse Venne for the plans of the present basilica. The first sketches of the Oratory date back to that period. They soon included the vast gardens at the bottom of the hill, the crypt-church and the large basilica crowned with a dome which was to be seen from 40 miles around. Saint Joseph's Oratory had become the project of a whole population gathered around the faith and prayer of Brother André.

He was now 69 years old. Walking briskly, he entered his office every morning at nine o'clock, to welcome the sick and all those in need. In spite of his poor health, he was amazingly active. From Monday through Thursday, at the end of his office hours, he again visited sick people at home in the company of one of his many friends.

Indeed he was for all an engaging personality; a simple man, yet alert and sensitive, profoundly interested in people and in their needs. Everybody loved him.

Brother André walking to his office on September 23, 1923.

VUE A VOL D'OISEAU DE LA BASILIQUE DE SAINT-JOSEPH AVEC LA CRYPTE ET LES CHAPELLES. — Ce
temple aera un superbe monument d'architecture du style de la renaissance italienne. Il aura la forme d'une
croix latine et aura 320 pieds de longueur.—Dessin des architectes Viau et Venne.

Caption in the Montreal daily paper LA PRESSE on May 13, 1916:

"BIRD'S EYE VIEW OF SAINT JOSEPH'S BASILICA, WITH THE CRYPT-
CHURCH AND CHAPELS. It will be a magnificent monument in the
Italian Renaissance style, 320 feet long, in the shape of a Latin cross.
Plan by architects Viau & Venne."

The marble statue of Saint Joseph by Italian artist A. Giacomini
stood in the Oratory's crypt church since December, 1917

A Humble Man's
Devotion To Saint Joseph

Canon Étienne Catta was a well-known writer and biographer of the Congregation of Holy Cross. He and his brother Tony wrote the life story of the Founder, Father Basil Moreau, that of the pastor who founded the *Brothers of Saint Joseph,* Father James Francis Dujarié, that of the first superior of the Holy Cross sisters, Léocadie Gascoin, and that of the first Canadian Holy Cross priest, Camille Lefebvre. In 1964 he also wrote a life story of Blessed Brother André.

Sister Léocadie Gascoin, M.S.C.

The general procurator of Holy Cross, Father Edward Heston — my superior when I was a seminarian — translated the Cattas' biographies of Father Moreau, Father Dujarié, and Sister Leocadie Gascoin. When that of Brother André was written, in 1964, Father Heston was in charge of communications for the English section of the press during the Vatican II Council. He later became an archbishop of the Roman curia and was appointed prefect of the Congregation for Social Communications. Therefore, Canon Catta's biography of Brother André was never translated into English.

The first part on Brother André's ancestry and the people of their time in the Province of Quebec is a bit lengthy. The second part on Brother André's youth and on his entry to the Congregation as a Holy Cross Brother is more interesting. Another part is on the development of his Oratory.

At that point in the book, one statement is somewhat amazing and is worthy of reflection.

Canon Catta wrote, "One could thus write on and on about the development of Saint Joseph's Oratory almost without ever mentioning the name Brother André." In other words, one could write pages upon pages about the Oratory, and everything that happened, and every decision that was made, almost without even mentioning the name of its founder.

Catta gave several examples of what he meant. When the property was purchased on top of Mount Royal, Brother André was never consulted. The purpose of the purchase was obviously not to build an Oratory. The fact was that the Congregation had long noticed the magnificent view from the hilltop and they feared that some noisy club might be established and disturb the pupils in the school.

The superiors had their views on the property and never thought of consulting with the doorkeeper. Brother André was behind the scenes, not making himself known as THE promoter of the Oratory.

Brother André with his confreres at the Oratory on September 18, 1927.

When the first chapel was built, lay people had to take charge; they donated the wood and contributed their time and skill so that the project would materialize. It was done with the help of Brother Abundius Piché, the school carpenter.

In 1908, another committee of lay people held meetings, then wrote a petition and got 2,000 signatures so that a new section could be added to the chapel. They made the arrangements so that the new building might be heated during the winter. Once again, they provided all the money, and their time and skill, for each new development to take place.

Of course Brother André was the inspiration of the whole venture, but somehow he stood in the background. As it seems, he was almost never involved in the actual process of decision-making. He always remained unassuming, and that was the case — maybe even more so — when the large basilica was built.

Officially he was appointed as a member of the council, but that did not seem to have much meaning at the time, given his position in the community. He knew what he wanted and insisted at times. But through it all, he remained the humble, weak and fragile little brother, the one who had already spent 40 years of his life as a doorkeeper, waiting in prayer, watering the flowers, doing some odd errands, and especially scrubbing the floors. Not at all a man in a position of leadership.

Actually everything took place because of him, and they all knew it. Had he not been there, nothing would have

Saint Joseph's Oratory rises 506 feet above street level, and 856 feet above average sea level. It is the highest point in Montreal.

happened on top of Mount Royal. One day, in his timid way, he had asked permission to make a very small wooden roof over a Saint Joseph statue which had been given to him by a friend, and which he wanted to set on the hilltop so as to help people pray. The superior never suspected that granting this harmless permission would grow into the largest shrine dedicated to Saint Joseph anywhere in the world, and that it would eventually attract more than 2,000,000 people every year!

That permission actually was given in the infirmary, when the superior was sick, and so was Brother André. Surely, the superior never realized the importance of the permission he gave at that moment. It sounds like a situation where a superior looked over his glasses, considered Brother André's request, found that it wouldn't harm anyone, nodded yes, and went back to reading his breviary.

But then Brother André's friends wanted a chapel, and then a shelter behind it, and some heating, and a restaurant, and everything followed almost by itself. It was Brother André's dream, but not his personal project. To him, clearly, IT WAS SAINT JOSEPH'S PROJECT.

Just as the work of Holy Cross, in Father Moreau's view, had to be the work of God, so in Brother André's view, all that happened on Mount Royal came from the Lord; and nothing came from his own efforts or from his own will. He himself was small, and weak, and sickly, but he loved to pray. Later his prayer was found so efficient that everybody wanted to pray with him. But he directed their attention to Saint Joseph, and through him, to the goodness of the Lord. So, it was not his work: IT WAS SAINT JOSEPH'S. And all HE could do was pray.

The Solemnity of Saint Joseph on May 11, 1924.

Simple Prayer

There was a lot of simplicity and humility in his prayer. He prayed like the old folks, in the very simple way he had been taught. Here are some of his practices, always connected with confident prayer:

He would use a medal of Saint Joseph in order to express his confidence. He would use some devotional oil from the lamp that burned in front of a statue of Saint Joseph. These practices were not always appreciated by members of the clergy, nor by all his confreres, nor by the wise and learned who sometimes laughed at these popular forms of prayer. That was a fact even 25 years after the founding of the original chapel. Brothers who are still alive today can remember hearing some of their confreres calling Brother André "The Old Fool of the Mountain!"

Diocesan authorities conducted an inquiry in November, 1910, and after four months, decided in favor of André and his work. However, their approval had not come at the end of a long canonical process. They had not reached the final conclusions that were established at the end of the trial for beatification. So in the mind of his contemporaries, the approval of Church authorities had remained quite debatable.

Still, it seems that no one could stop this popular movement of prayer based on signs given by the Lord, a movement of prayer for the glory of God. The movement, so to speak, of a whole nation discerning more and more

A temporary annex was used while the crypt-church was built.

clearly the special protection that came from the saint who, after Mary, was really the closest to the Lord. No one, in fact, could resist, or even oppose a prayer movement which rose like a cry of misery from the mouths of hundreds of believers, and that became more and more like an immense song of hope.

What made the superiors consider the Oratory seriously, and what made them see the importance of investing more energy and more resources in the venture, was the fact that André himself never showed any personal pride in all that was taking place. It soon became the project of hundreds and then of thousands of believers. So it rested upon a very broad popular basis.

Officially and publicly, during solemn Masses or other large gatherings of people, the superiors and bishops only hinted at the role played by Brother André since the beginning. They would talk about him, never mentioning his name. And the amazing thing is that everyone understood except André himself, who always thought they were speaking about Saint Joseph, who had initiated the project.

Although everyone knew Brother André had started the venture, it soon became the work of everyone: superiors, benefactors, builders, managers, everyone joined the project "for the glory of God" and "for the glory of Saint Joseph,"

and André himself gave all the credit to his friend, Saint Joseph.

His Devotion to Saint Joseph

His devotion to his favorite saint was his light and the stronghold of his humility. After his death, witnesses came to realize that he never talked much about his youth,

Alfred Bessette at the age of 12.

The statue in the crypt-church.

except to very special friends. Only a few of them could say, during the trial for beatification, "Brother André told me that he ALWAYS HAD this great devotion to Saint Joseph, which he had received from his mother." As it seems, his mother had been chosen by the Lord to give her son a devotion which would then flourish on Mount Royal. Even before he was a teenager, his companions at St. Cesaire used to say, "He's going crazy with his devotion to Saint Joseph." This remark, obnoxious though it is, reveals a lot about the prayer of Alfred Bessette as a youngster: "He's going crazy with his devotion to Saint Joseph."

Years later, nothing had changed. He still spent hours before the statue of Saint Joseph, and some people still laughed at him. But he so loved the Lord and his Saint, that he kept believing and praying. He also kept on comforting those in need. A witness said: "Brother André spoke constantly about Saint Joseph. He recommended invoking him and having confidence in him."

The advice he gave to everyone was almost trivial: "Pray to Saint Joseph, and I'll pray with you." He said this to thousands of people. Day after day, year after year, they came back with the same recommendation: "Pray to Saint Joseph and have confidence in him. I will pray with you."

So much so that many people said André did not say much about Saint Joseph. Only to special friends, did he speak much about Saint Joseph's life or about his role as husband of Mary and earthly father of Jesus. Nor did he say much about the virtues of Saint Joseph, even though he was delighted every time he heard priests and theologians speak about such things in church.

What comes out of his daily conversations with people, even out of his trust and his practices was a very simple fact: "Saint Joseph is a human being who has lived our experiences. He is a friend of ours, and he is living with God. Saint Joseph was sent to the Church much in the same way that he was sent to Jesus and Mary, in order to secure the material and spiritual good of God's family." And that role applied especially to the poor, the sick, the sinners, all those who suffer, who trust in the Lord, and take the time to pray. Saint Joseph is a personal friend living with God and with the Church — he is a personal defender against evil — he is the protector of the Church against all dangers of the present time.

Brother André's message could thus be summarized as one broad invitation: GO TO SAINT JOSEPH. And the result was a very simple form of prayer. As one witness recalled, "He recommended very simple forms of prayer like: 'Saint Joseph, pray for me as you yourself would have prayed if you had been in my place, in the same situation. Saint Joseph, hear me!'"

And he kept repeating this: "When you invoke Saint Joseph, you don't have to speak much. You know your

Father in heaven knows what you need; well, so does his friend Saint Joseph."

"Go before a statue of Saint Joseph. Tell him: 'If you were in my place, Saint Joseph, what would you do? What would you want to be done to you? Well, pray for this in my behalf!'"

"Saint Joseph, see, I am the father of a large family. Please help me, like you would have liked others to help you, if you had been in the same situation on earth."

Plaques and crutches in the chapel.

At times, Brother André spoke about Saint Joseph in a more meditative form. He talked about the experiences of Saint Joseph, his problems and his trials, but always in the company of Christ. And so, according to André, Saint Joseph lived in a constant, daily relationship with God. This DAILY RELATIONSHIP WITH GOD is paramount with Brother André, and it is what he wanted people to do now. In other words, he invited people to live in the presence of God, just like Mary and Joseph had lived in Nazareth in the daily presence of the Lord, whatever the problems or the situation.

Brother André invited people to pray in traditional ways which simple believers could use. One was to write a short prayer on a piece of paper and to leave it under the statue of Saint Joseph. These prayers were very simple and direct forms like: "Saint Joseph, come to help me. I don't now how to pray. What would you do if you were in my place? Please, do it for me now." And he would slip the paper under the statue of Saint Joseph.

A winter Sunday.

A Novena

André's own prayer frequently took the form of the novena, and he often advised others, "Pray to Saint Joseph. Make a novena to Saint Joseph." The point of nine days of prayer was not to say long prayers, or even a large number of prayers, or to say any prayer in particular, but to insist with confidence and perseverance in prayer.

What is striking about a novena is that it is essentially a popular devotion, a popular form of prayer. Nowhere in the liturgy — the official prayer of the Church: the mass and the breviary — do we find a novena. Three days are a biblical figure for a very special prayer, and in the liturgy we find the three days of prayer, during the spring, for a good harvest. A novena seems to be three times three days. And all it means is a very persistent and a very insistent prayer.

Though novenas have never been put officially into the liturgy, Christians have made them for centuries. Those who have tried it know what perseverance it takes to go to church nine days in a row, or nine Sundays in a row, in order to obtain a special favor. It is not biblical, nor liturgical, but it is a most traditional form of prayer in the Christian Church.

During the late 1970's, when we were preparing the many documents requested for Brother André's beatification, we read many pages of what other postulators had written and found that many of the miracles recognized by the Church took place after a novena. Everywhere in the world, when a person has a very special intention, he or she will make a novena. And the Lord seems to approve of this practice, since many of the major miracles obtained through prayer, and officially acknowledged by the Church, were granted after a novena.

The Medal

Brother André also told people to use a medal. He said not only to wear it, but also to use it as a way of expressing their faith and confidence. "A man is not a walking brain," he would explain. "We need to see, and to touch, and to feel." And he would say, "Make a novena, and rub yourself with a medal of Saint Joseph." He said this to thousands of people, according to the witnesses.

The interior of the crypt-church today.

Some hesitated about a prayer that was so physical, as they shunned superstition. Matthew, Mark and Luke, however, each told the story of the woman who had suffered from hemorrhage during 12 years, and whose only prayer consisted in touching the Lord's garment. Jesus made no mistake about it; he said to the woman, "Your FAITH has saved you!" [1]

Brother André himself used lots of medals. The one he used the most was a rather large one, representing on the one side, Saint Joseph holding the Child Jesus, and on the other side, Saint Joseph's Oratory. In the beginning, some people accused him of spreading superstition and making people believe in magic. Once André heard of it, he insisted more and more that the medal was a sign of faith, an expression of our confidence in God.

---

(1) Matt. 9:22 ; Mark 5:34 ; Luke 8:48.

He had a keen sense of psychology and he knew how much people like to keep a souvenir. The medal he gave them became precious in every family. And they used it a lot. He could not bless the medals, but he was intelligent enough to realize that people were pleased to have received one from him. And he gave very many of them. Witnesses said that when he traveled, he always had a large number of medals in his pockets and he would give them out in profusion, insisting that people use them with confidence along with prayer. He did the same when he visited the sick in hospitals or in their homes.

Whenever someone had some difficulty to work out, he said, "Take a medal of Saint Joseph with you, and hold it in your hand while you're talking. Saint Joseph will help you." Holding a medal was for him almost like holding Saint Joseph's hand.

The Oil

Another practice Brother André recommended was the use of devotional oil: "Rub yourself with a medal of Saint Joseph and with Saint Joseph's oil." The idea of associating the use of olive oil with prayer comes from the Bible. In Saint Mark's Gospel (6:13), when the Apostles were sent on their first mission, they "anointed many sick people and the sick were healed." The same idea is found in the Epistle of James (5:14), "If one of you is sick, let him call the elders of the Church, and let them pray for him after anointing him with oil in the name of the Lord."

When he entered the community, Brother André learned how devotional oil was used in the early tradition of Holy Cross. The founder, Father Moreau, had a close friend who used oil. He was Leon Dupont, the Holy Man of Tours, whose cause for beatification was also introduced in Rome. This layman went to Le Havre in 1841 with Fa-  ther Edward Sorin and the first Holy Cross missionaries to make arrangements for their sea voyage to the United States. Father Moreau consulted Dupont whenever he had a difficult affair to negotiate. Following a European custom, Dupont often removed olive oil from the lamp that burned in front of his very cherished image of the Holy Face of Jesus and used it to anoint the sick; and miracles happened.

A similar case is found in the early chronicles of Holy Cross in Canada. One day a sister postulant became sick after catching cold in a heavy rain storm. After she had entered the novitiate, her fever developed into pneumonia which brought her to the point where the doctor said he could do nothing. Father Kilroy, C.S.C., gave the sisters some of the oil which the Holy Man of Tours had given to him, and the nurse prayed with confidence as she rubbed the back of the young woman. Much to her amazement and that of the community, the young sister recovered instantly and completely.

BROTHER ANDRE'S ROOM

This miracle happened in July of 1851, at the time when the sisters, brothers and priests still belonged to the one same community and we can be sure that Brother André heard about this well-known fact when he joined the Congregation of Holy Cross.

On the feast of Saint Joseph, five years before the construction of the original chapel, the chronicles report that Brother André spent one hour in chapel, distributing bottles of Saint Joseph's oil. Afterwards, he arranged that a lamp be

The chapel of Notre Dame School was completed in 1889.

The crowned statue of Saint Joseph blessed by Saint Pius X in 1909.

put in front of the statue of Saint Joseph in his own doorkeeper's cell. Thus he could readily give some oil to visitors who came to the door.

Here is what some of the witnesses said about the oil after Brother André had died:

"In 1905, I was sick and 36 years old. So I called upon Brother André, and he came to see me. He prayed with me. He gave me some of Saint Joseph's oil to drink — for I had pain in my stomach. I drank a sip of oil, and the next day there was a big improvement."

"In 1912, a little girl came who was about to lose one eye after an accident. Brother André gave her some Saint Joseph's oil, and she recovered just as he had promised."

"In 1916, a young brother in formation suffered with eczema. The superior brought him to see Brother André. 'What is this?' André asked. 'I have eczema,' the young brother answered, 'and the doctor says he can do nothing.' 'Rub yourself with this medal,' said Brother André, 'and use some of this oil. There is nothing like Saint Joseph to help you!' The young brother said afterwards, 'I went to bed and did exactly what Brother André had said. And on the following day, the eczema had totally disappeared. I have been well ever since.'"

"In 1931, a two-year-old crippled child was brought to Brother André. Both his legs were so twisted and his feet so deformed he could not walk. He too was healed after his parents rubbed his legs with Saint Joseph's oil. His parents were most grateful, for they had prayed since the day of his birth."

Saint Joseph's medal and Saint Joseph's oil may well be the practices Brother André recommended the most often; and he did it right from the beginning, as the doorkeeper of Notre Dame School. He also took the time to explain that this was not magic or superstition. As witnesses reported, he explained: "The oil and the medal help us think of Saint Joseph; they support our confidence in him."

With the young brothers, he insisted: "We should always invoke our special patron Saint Joseph. We only invoke him when we are sick. We should always pray."

Confidence

If there is any feeling involved in prayer, according to Brother André, it has to be confidence. In the tradition of Father Dujarié and Father Moreau, Brother André was taught

Father James F. Dujarié.

to trust in Divine Providence. *"Deus Providebit,"* was
Father Dujarié's motto: "God Will Provide." Even Father
Moreau repeated this very often. For Brother André,
confidence in God and confidence in his friend Saint Joseph
were one and the same thing. So he said about God and
Saint Joseph: "They will see and find a solution." And
oftentimes he would associate the name of Mary in this
prayer, saying: "Saint Joseph has great power over the
heart of God, with his wife, the Virgin Mary." All these
words are found time and again in what the witnesses have
told during the trial for beatification.

Another witness said Brother André repeated: "Pray to
Saint Joseph, and he will never leave you along the way."
Once again, confidence was the rule.

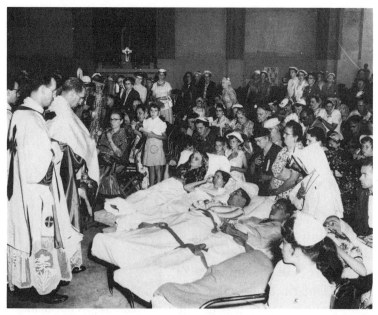

"People who suffer have something to offer to the good God." André.

When a healing took place or some other favor was obtained, he said: "Thank you, Saint Joseph! Thank you, Saint Joseph!" And he told everyone what great favors his good friend had obtained from the Almighty. He knew his prayer was heard, and he spent his whole life teaching people confidence in prayer.

When reading all these lines in the very words of the witnesses during the beatification process, one might wonder, "Why did he invoke Saint Joseph so much instead of praying directly to God?"

Actually, Brother André's faith was rooted in the Gospel, and his prayer was Catholic and universal. "His principal devotion," repeated some of his closest friends, "was to the Passion of the Lord. In fact, Brother André always taught us not to separate a true devotion to the Blessed Mother from that to Saint Joseph, and, especially, to Our Lord." Since the novitiate, he had learned about the special devotions of the Congregation, especially devotion to the Holy Family. He also inherited all the major devotions of the 19th century: the Sacred Heart, the Holy Face, the Precious Blood of Jesus. Brother André was pious, and all these appealed to him.

Also, according to a witness, "Brother André spoke often about the Blessed Trinity. He recalled the goodness of the Father, who has given us his Only Son. He recommended that we pray to the Holy Spirit, and that we ask him to enlighten our hearts and our minds when we have important decisions to make."

One very close friend of Brother André even declared under oath, "He almost never spoke to me about Saint

Joseph, because he knew I love him well. Instead, he would speak to me about the Blessed Mother and the Sacred Heart."

Intentions for Prayer

Brother André's intentions for prayer were also broader than those of his usual visitors, who wanted the healing of a wound, the strengthening of one leg, the recovery of a blind person, or even the conversion of a sinner. He also prayed for the major intentions of the Church at that time, and the intentions of the Pope, especially with the rise of communism in Europe. He prayed and asked people to pray for peace and freedom among the nations.

The role of Brother André in the development of Saint Joseph's Oratory, as well as in helping the Church spread the devotion to Saint Joseph — not only in Canada but also in the United Stated and in the world — comes out clearly in what the witnesses said during the process for beatification in the early 1940's, not very long after he had died.

Indeed, the French missionaries chose Saint Joseph as the special Patron of Canada in 1624; but it was often said that all their efforts, as well as those of other priests and bishops, never succeeded so much as Brother André's endeavor to make Saint Joseph better known and loved.

In doing that, Brother André did not act on his own. He belonged to a congregation dedicated to spreading devotion to the Holy Family. However, the decision of the brothers and priests serving at Saint Joseph's Oratory would not have been sufficient to achieve the same result.

On this particular point, the superior general of Holy Cross, Father James W. Donahue, went to Montreal to see for himself what was going on with Brother André. Father Donahue had spent most of his life in formation ministry and was a fervent man, who wanted every member of the Congregation to develop a solid piety and a deep spiritual life.

When he came to Canada for the canonical visitation, he was particularly interested in seeing that a well-balanced piety would grow everywhere. After his visit, he was happy to report that the influence of Brother André, and of the community serving at the Oratory, had a very good balance and a precise sense of religious values.

Saint Joseph's Oratory in 1932.

Father Donahue found that devotion to the Lord clearly had the first place at the Oratory, followed by a solid devotion to Mary; and he found nothing, as he had feared, of a predominant or distorted devotion to Saint Joseph. Father Donahue's conclusion was therefore that it was Jesus and Mary who had agreed to spread a devotion worthy of the Head of the Holy Family, through the efforts of Holy Cross;

The original chapel in March, 1918. See caption on page 157.

and he wrote in his report, "Little Brother André alone could never have achieved such a great work."

With an extraordinary zeal, Brother André devoted his life to spreading devotion to Saint Joseph everywhere, yet he called himself: "Saint Joseph's Little Dog." And he smiled because he knew clearly that he had been an underdog all his life. And deep down in his heart, he knew that ALL THIS WAS GOD'S WORK, NOT HIS.

A bird's eye view of Saint Joseph's Oratory today.

The design of the arches in the basilica was based on fingers joining in prayer. The Little Singers of Mount Royal (top) sing masterworks from the Renaissance to the present day during Sunday Mass at 11:00.

Christian Devotions

Brother André's devotion to Saint Joseph was well known. He himself claimed he owed it to his mother; during family prayer, she invoked the protector of Jesus for every need. As we have seen in the previous chapter, it also became the stronghold of his humility.

However witnesses have pointed out several other devotions, and it would be wrong to single out one of them without taking into account many other dimensions of André's prayer. Let us first consider what a Christian devotion is, and describe the social milieu in which André found his various forms of prayer. His spiritual life will then appear in a better perspective.

Christian Devotion

"Devotio" is a Latin word which originally referred to a pagan custom of casting a spell by "devoting," or giving up a person entirely to the gods of Hades. It was a way either to appease them or to obtain their favors.

The first Christians, however, used this word to describe the total submission and radical belonging of every being to the one true God. It was the first religious act, the perfect adoration of God as Creator, one Lord, and absolute Master of all things. "Devoting" oneself to God, or surrendering totally to him, without reservation, was the one and only Christian "devotion" in the first sense of the word.

Centuries later, for instance in the Flemish monasteries of the 13th century, the word took on another meaning. The monks insisted that love was the center of Christian life. From then on, a "devotion" became a movement of the heart and soul towards God and the saints. A new distinction began to be made between the liturgy, the official prayer of the Church which was celebrated in Latin, and popular "devotions" which spoke more directly to the people. Devotion to the Passion of Christ became widespread in the 12th and 13th centuries, while the rosary also became more and more popular.

Since then several practices developed as devotions to the Holy Face, the Five Wounds, and the Precious Blood of Jesus. Still closer to us a Chilean priest, Father Mateo Crawley, spread devotion to the Sacred Heart in Europe and in Latin America during and after the First World War.

Some looked on such devotions as derivatives of the liturgy which sprang up because it was in Latin. Some others saw them as a secondary form of piety based on images rather than on faith.

Let us consider a few examples of this. The life story of Saint George — the Roman soldier who saved a young woman from the fangs of the dragon — is one of the most obscure in all of Christianity. Yet, his image of a valiant knight holding his spear against a dragon is a beautiful image of our victory against evil; so he became an object of an unceasing cult, and countless icons of him were painted in the Eastern Churches of Egypt, Palestine, Greece and

Saint George and the dragon.

Russia. Many European cities chose him as their patron saint and had his image cut into stone; England made him patron of the kingdom. In a similar way, people invoked Saint Christopher without knowing him, since all that is known about him is pure legend. The Pastor of Ars spread a similar devotion to Saint Philomena, whose very existence was so dubious that her feast day was removed from the calendar. During the 19th century, a strange devotion began to Saint Expedit, a Turkish martyr from the 4th century. By playing on words, people were led to believe that his intercession was "expeditious" and they have invoked him for urgent matters ever since.

Obviously, these popular "devotions" are a secondary form of piety, and many efforts were made to explain them with a lot of patience and care. The fact that the feast of Saint George is still in the calendar on

Saint Expedit.

April 23, shows how much the Church respects popular representations.

Devotion and the Christian Mystery

If we narrow down the concept, a Christian devotion may also be well rooted in faith. Then it answers a human need to emphasize certain aspects of the Gospel in order to support a popular movement of faith and conversion. In this sense, Christian devotions answer some more specific needs of a culture, an era, or a country. Certain devotions are more essential, like the one to the Sacred Heart or to Mary, because they touch the very core of the Christian Mystery.

As it is proclaimed in the Apostles' Creed and after the Consecration, the Christian Mystery is Christ in his work of salvation; Jesus bringing all humanity back to his Father, into the unity of the Spirit, and in view of the Kingdom. It is the acclamation of the Christian assembly: "Christ has died, Christ is risen, Christ will come again." Or according to a more developed form: "Christ has come, Christ was born, Christ has suffered, Christ has died, Christ is risen, Christ is alive, Christ will come again, Christ dwells among us."

Now, each element of the Christian Mystery may well give way to an authentic devotion. For instance, the sight of Christ on the Cross may involve the Christian "devotion" in its full sense, since it intimately unites a believer to Jesus who was crucified, died, and rose again for us. The Cross as it was contemplated by Saint Paul [1] is therefore the

---

(1) Letter to the Philippians 2:6-11.

central core of every devotion and has become the sign, the symbol par excellence of all Christians.

Crucifix by Henri Charlier.

Brother André, a Brother of Holy Cross, gave us several examples of this unity in Christian devotion. In his prayer, as his biographer Canon Catta observed, the mystery of the Incarnation — that of the Holy Family — was connected to the one of the Redemption. Mary gave Jesus to the world, and Joseph was his guardian on earth. Their mission was to help him prepare for his own mission as Savior of the world. After sharing his life on earth, Mary and Joseph shared also in his glory as Risen Lord. Therefore, all the graces they obtained flowed from the one same Christian Mystery.

Brother André's Milieu

Before we consider the various aspects of Brother André's devotion, it would be wise to briefly describe the social milieu in which he grew up. One cannot appreciate the spiritual life of his time without at least a few notions of history and culture.

The first permanent European settlement in Canada dates back to 1603, four years before the first British settlement in Jamestown, Virginia. Canada, however, was a French colony and remained so for 156 years — until shortly before the American Revolution. When the British won the so-called French and Indian War in 1759, they also took over Canada. So Alfred Bessette grew up in the aftermath of the British conquest.

André's birthplace near St. Gregoire, 30 miles southeast of Montreal.

In 1760, the white population on the shores of the St. Lawrence River consisted of about 70,000 people. But it was growing fast, especially because of large families. By and large, it was French-speaking and Catholic.

The British imposed on civil servants an oath of fidelity that practically denied the Catholic faith. This stirred up opposition between the two cultures, and most of the learned French people, like the attorneys, judges, officers, lawyers — all those with an education and a bit of money — left the country.

Historians agree that the French had brought their institutions to America. The school system in Canada, in 1760, compared well with the one in France. But in the following 80 years, three generations were practically

The College of the Jesuits in Quebec City in 1759.

deprived of schools and only a few boys were taught by local pastors. Alfred's mother, Clothilde Foisy, was given private lessons in her thriving home-town of

Clothilde Foisy

Clothilde's signature on the day of her marriage.

Chambly. Later she taught her child how to read and write. That is why André could read out loud from a book, when he conducted the Holy Hour with his friends in the new crypt-church of the Oratory in 1919. The fact that he knew how to read was above average in his day and age.

Four years before Alfred's birth in 1845, the British Parliament in London overturned a decision made by the local Government, and the Catholic Church was finally able to conduct its own French-speaking schools. That very year

102   *Brother André*

Bishop Ignatius
Bourget of Montreal
went to see Father
Basil Moreau in
LeMans, France, to
ask for teaching
brothers. The found-
er of Holy Cross
explained to him
that he could not
send the brothers
alone since the
special purpose of
his congregation
was that the sisters,
brothers and priests
work together. The
bishop argued that he

Father Basil A. Moreau, C.S.C.
(1799-1873)

had his own Canadian sisters; but they finally came to an
agreement, and eight brothers, four sisters and two priests
of Holy Cross arrived in Canada in the spring of 1847.
They were to help rebuild the Catholic school system at a
time when 90% of the people did not even know how to sign
their own names.

Oral Culture

So when Alfred Bessette joined Holy Cross, he belonged to this oral culture in which people depended a lot on their
memory. He never dreamt of becoming a teaching brother.
As a novice, he followed the program then designed for

those who were illiterate or without formal schooling. Among other things, these novices had to learn by heart chapters 5, 6 and 7 of Saint Matthew: the Sermon on the Mount.

Alfred, though unschooled, was talented; one could even say he was bright. He was endowed with a quick mind, a keen sense of humor, and a very dependable memory. Therefore he learned the Sermon on the Mount easily. And as he began to better understand and to love the Word of God, he went on learning by heart the parables, Jesus' miracles, and a number of other excerpts, especially the whole section on the Passion, which he could recount in detail. By and large, he knew more excerpts from the Gospel by heart than many a priest, and that is one reason why he was so well rooted in the Gospel. It was the result of his culture on the one hand, and of the formation he had as a Brother of Holy Cross on the other.

Holy Cross Tradition

Only 16 days after Alfred Bessette arrived in Cote-des-Neiges to begin his postulancy, Pope Pius IX proclaimed the Guardian of the Redeemer as the Protector of the Universal Church. The Pope was following a well-established tradition: "Saint Joseph has protected Christ, he can also protect his body, which is the Church." Numerous articles were published, and there is no doubt that the young brothers who entered in André's time heard a lot on the role of their Patron Saint in the Christian Mystery.

An older priest, Father Narcisse Hupier, C.S.C., also had a profound influence on André during his last months of novitiate. As a diocesan priest, Father Hupier had served as chaplain to Father Dujarié's Brothers of Saint Joseph; then both he and they joined Father Moreau's Congregation of Holy Cross.

In 1872, Father Hupier was sent to Canada and stayed in the same house with André. This priest had such a reputation as a saint that, when he died in New Brunswick, the Acadian people stole his body before it could be shipped to Montreal and buried him in their own soil. Brother André followed one of his retreats and remembered him all his life as a living witness of the foundation of Holy Cross, and a wonderful priest.

His Main Devotion: The Passion

"Devotion to Saint Joseph was not Brother André's predominant devotion. Indeed, his main devotion was to the Passion of Our Lord Jesus Christ."

This surprising statement by André's biographer, Canon Étienne Catta, is supported by the very best witnesses.

"His predominant devotion", said the first witness, "was to the Passion of Our Lord.... He often recommended praying to the Sacred Heart; he had a remarkable veneration for the Precious Blood of Jesus." Whenever he wanted to speak very seriously with a sinner, he would tell in detail the story of the Passion. "All the devotions he had, always seemed to be based on his devotion to the Passion of Our Lord," said the same first witness. "The mystery of the Passion is that on which he meditated the most in his personal prayer, and about which he often spoke."

Those who had heard André talk about the Passion said they were so impressed they remembered his words the rest of their lives.

Indeed Brother André was, in his own way, a storyteller. Sometimes he would tell the whole life story of Jesus, begin-

The Twelfth Station
in the Oratory's gardens.

ning with his birth. At other times, he recounted the parables, which he had learned by heart, but told in his own words. The first witness, who knew Brother André very well for 25 years, said that he could tell the whole life story of Our Lord. But as he mentioned, Brother André would speak above all about the Passion.

That was well within his culture, it was well within his time, and it was well within the tradition of Holy Cross.

According to the witnesses, when he spoke about the Passion, his face would change. And he would give all the details as though he himself had been present. He would tell the story of the High Priest, of Pontius Pilate, the 39 lashes. And then he followed the sequence of the Stations of the Cross: how Jesus met his Mother, how he had become the suffering Servant of the Lord, how he was nailed by the hands and by the feet.

But he always found his own words, his own way of telling such a well-known story, filled it with emotions as though he had been there and fully realized what was going on. As one witness said, "He spoke about the Passion as though he was living every detail; and when you looked at his face, you could tell he was suffering along with Jesus."

Another thing the witnesses said was that they never got tired of listening to him as he told the story of the Passion. One said, "I listened to him twice as he told the story of the Passion, which could take two hours. And I wished I had the opportunity to listen to him a third time, but I didn't dare ask."

Another one said: "When Brother André started talking about the Passion, he would never end."

One day a man invited him to his country house. Brother André, knowing this man did not lead a very good life, started telling him the story of the Passion. "Everyone gathered around him," said the witness, "and it lasted three hours. Everyone listened and everyone was moved. When

Brother André ended, the man thanked him with tears in his eyes."

Unfortunately, no recording was made and nobody took notes. The witnesses remembered only some of his words like: "The love which Our Lord had during his Passion puts into full light God's love for us." Obviously, the purpose of Brother André, in telling the story of the Passion, was to bring everyone to answer this love.

October 8, 1925.

He did it many times, according to the witnesses; they used the words "frequently" and even "constantly." Those who were fortunate enough to listen several times to him as he told the story of the Passion said it was never boring. "Every time," they said, "we learned something new." On the other hand, Brother André was aware that his listeners were encouraged after having heard about the sufferings of Our Lord and that they went back reconciled and more ready to cope with their everyday struggles.

A priest also remembered that, when Brother André went to see him in his room, oftentimes he would talk to him about the Passion. He would recite by heart entire excerpts from the Gospel, sometimes with tears in his eyes.

September 3, 1916.

He would tell everyone that they should have a crucifix in their house and when a statue was more visible than the crucifix, he would point out the fact to his friends. This is one more reason why the witnesses said that the Passion of Our Lord was Brother André's main devotion.

The Word of God

Another devotion of Brother André was the Word of God. As we have said before, during his novitiate those who were not trained to teach oftentimes did not know how to read and write. Their culture was an oral one, and their memory was usually better than ours because they had to depend on it every day.

During the novitiate, André memorized the Sermon on the Mount just like the others, but since he knew how to read and had so enjoyed learning the Sermon on the Mount, he decided to memorize also most of "The Four Gospels in One," a book which put into one continuous narrative excerpts from Saint Matthew, Saint Mark, Saint Luke and Saint John. For the Passion, however, he learned by heart the narrative from each of the four Gospels separately so that he was able to put them together into one single story.

So, when he talked to the people during his lifetime, especially when people asked for his advice, he often quoted the Gospel. The Word of God was his favorite reading and his favorite meditation, and when talking to his friends, he would share with them thoughts from his last meditation.

April 19, 1927.

An exercise which would be very much in line with the spirituality of André would be the reading of one of the Gospels in a single evening since such a practice gives the reader an overall view of the life of Jesus as well as a better sense of the purpose of each Evangelist.

After the Passion, the pages of the Gospel André spoke of most were the parables on compassion and mercy. He talked a lot about the prodigal son, the lost sheep, the miraculous catch of fish, the multiplication of the loaves.

He would tell his friends, "Here, I have found something interesting for you. It will do you some good." Of course, the page was well known, but it was read anew, as though it were for the first time. Then he would say, "It's not sufficient to read it once — you must read it again when you're alone."

He was very happy and would tell others when people came back to him and shared what they had understood in a second or in a third reading.

The Eucharist

In addition to his devotion to the Passion of Our Lord, and to the Word of God, Brother André had a remarkable

In the original chapel about 1906.

devotion to the Eucharist. Especially during the first years of the original chapel, he served Mass for almost every priest who came.

Even during the years that followed, when he was increasingly active, he would usually take the time to attend Mass twice or three times every morning. Prayer was obviously an important activity for him. Mass was in Latin and most often it was an early and a silent Mass. He attended from his pew, behind the altar, and considered this a precious moment in his day. He told his friends that during Mass he offered his work and his difficulties in union with Our Lord in his Passion.

André went to communion every day, and all remembered how he spent time in profound union with the Lord present within him. During his frequent illnesses, he asked to receive communion in bed, and it was always followed by the same time of thanksgiving. When he was traveling, he regularly attended Mass, and when there was only one Mass, he would spend a half to three quarters of an hour as his personal time of thanksgiving.

The Tabernacle

His devotion to the Blessed Sacrament was just as remarkable. He spent much time before the tabernacle in a dialogue with the Lord. Sometimes he would say he was going to pray for five minutes. But once he was there, his visit would often last an hour or more.

A witness said, "Each time I saw Brother André in prayer before the Blessed Sacrament, I had the impression that he was profoundly absorbed in his prayer." Another one said, "Each time I had to go and disturb him in his pew, I had the impression that I was taking him away from an important conversation with God; and therefore, I always tried to leave him alone as long as I could."

When he was on vacation, he spent even more time in the local church. When he could be alone, he liked to kneel at the communion rail or even, when he was sure he was alone, on the lower step of the altar, with his arms crossed and nothing on which to lean. He had practiced this a long time and he could easily stay there motionless for hours. That is also how he prayed in the early years, in the original chapel: he knelt upright without a kneeler. He did the same every evening after coming back from his visits to the sick.

The Stations of the Cross

André's devotions to the Passion of Our Lord and to the Eucharist, added to his care of others, brought him to a practice that went on for years at the Oratory: the Holy Hour and the Stations of the Cross every Friday night.

The Stations of the Cross in the Oratory's gardens fulfilled one of
André's fondest dreams. They were completed in 1956.

It all started when he invited a handful of friends to pray
with him in his visit to the chapel at the end of the day. Fire
Chief Raoul Gauthier told that story to a journalist only a
few years later:

"It was in 1919. I came twice on a Friday evening, and
I realized that this was the time when Brother André made
his Holy Hour. So I told a few officers in my squad about
it; and by the following Friday, we had a small group of men
praying with him. This lasted two years.

"Then more and more people wanted to pray with
Brother André and joined the group. They in turn invited

members of their families and friends. At the end of the Holy Hour, we attended the Stations of the Cross led by Brother André. Then the diocesan authorities granted us permission to have the Exposition of the Blessed Sacrament."

Different groups and choirs volunteered to come and sing, and those who came once wanted to come again. People were very much impressed. As the crypt had been built only the year before, Brother André did not yet have his pew behind the altar. So he used one pew in the middle of the church and felt very much at ease with his friends. He would light a candle, let a few drops of wax fall on the edge of the pew and stick the candle there.

The interior of the crypt-church in the 1920's.

It all began with a half-hour reading on the Passion of Our Lord, a slow, meditative reading done by Brother André himself. For the next half hour, one of his friends would take the book and do the reading because Brother André's voice was weakening. Then they prayed the litany of the Sacred Heart, for which Brother André had a great devotion. Three, four, or five people attended at the beginning. They remained in the dark, except for the lamp in the sanctuary and Brother André's candle.

Only four years later, 126 people were there and signed a petition to the bishop so that the Blessed Sacrament could be exposed. The bishop answered, "You may expose the Blessed Sacrament, if at least 200 people attend!" The first time they did, 400 people were there, and the number kept increasing.

The Sacred Heart

In one of her visions at Paray-le-Monial, Saint Margaret Mary wrote the following message from the Sacred Heart: "In the night between Thursday and Friday, I will call you to take part in the mortal sadness I felt in the Garden of Olives, a sadness which will bring you close to an agony more bitter than death. So you will accompany me in the humble prayer I will offer to my Father. You will wake up between 11 o'clock and midnight to bow before me during one hour... you will beg mercy for sinners, so as to sweeten somehow the bitterness I felt when my apostles abandoned me and I told them they could not stay awake one hour to pray with me."

We don't know if Brother André ever read this well-known text written by Saint Margaret Mary in the second half of the 17th century. But as we go back in history, we can find the connection between André's two devotions, the Holy Hour and the Stations of the Cross.

He loved another book by a Visitation sister in Chambery, Marie Marthe Chambon, who wrote about the Sacred Heart, just like Saint Margaret Mary. But she connected the Holy Hour with her devotion to the Five Wounds of Jesus. Brother André also united both his devotions as one continuous prayer: the Holy Hour is the Agony as a prelude to the Condemnation by Pontius Pilate followed by the Stations of the Cross.

The feast of Saint Joseph on March 19, 1924.

We are amazed when we think that Brother André's friends stayed with him for at least one and a half, and maybe two hours. It certainly shows the influence he had on them. And it seems they loved it. It was beautiful: Brother André went from one station to the next, meditating out loud on each station, without a book. In fact, he had several books on the Stations of the Cross, and a lot to say about each station without repeating the same ideas. Later, when several hundred people attended, a priest conducted the prayer service.

Spreading These Devotions

In private conversations, Brother André dwelt on the love of Our Lord, on his Passion, and on the Holy Eucharist. The way he knelt in the church and for communion was in itself an incentive for others. But he also wanted to speak about these devotions. His visitors often quoted him as saying, "Go to communion. Go often to communion." Or else, "Our Lord cannot deny you a favor when he is present in your heart. Go find in him your strength, your joy, your consolation." Brother André always tried to convince people, and he did it with his charity and love. He also talked about everyone's concerns: their health, their business, their family. "But he always ended by talking about Mass and communion."

"Communion is the life of your soul. If you were to eat only one meal each week, would you survive?" he would ask. "It's the same thing with your soul: you must nourish your soul with the Holy Eucharist." And he would say, "There is a beautiful table set up in front of us, with great food on it. But sometimes we don't even bother to take it!"

The Virgin Mary

One of the well-known witnesses during Brother André's beatification process was the former superior general of Holy Cross, Father Albert F. Cousineau. He was Brother André's last superior at the end of his life, and later became a bishop in Haiti. As a witness during the process for beatification, he spoke especially about André's devotion to Mary.

"He had a great love for the Virgin Mary, and a very great devotion to her," Cousineau said.

The most visible sign of this devotion was that he always had his rosary in his hand whenever he had time to pray, walking from the residence to his office, or from his office to the chapel or the crypt. Witnesses remembered that he was actually praying. If they wanted to talk to him,

Albert F. Cousineau, C.S.C.

they knew he would take a few seconds in order to finish one Hail Mary, or a decade of his rosary.

When he visited the sick, he prayed the rosary with his driver, in the car. Then he continued on his own, especially when he traveled long distances. After he came back from his visits to the sick, he prayed for a while in the crypt-church. When the weather was nice, he and his driver walked back and forth in front of the Oratory and prayed another rosary together.

Brother André also loved to talk about Mary. "She is the Mother of God," he would say with admiration. Or else, "We must love the Blessed Virgin, for she is the Mother of

Our Lord Jesus Christ." He also called her, "Our Mother in Heaven."

This is also a devotion he inherited from his mother Clothilde, who loved him so much, and whom he loved very much. When he was small, he would pray the rosary with her, his little fingers following on the same beads she had just held in her fingers. Obviously, his love for his mother later developed into a relationship with the Virgin Mary.

"If you consider all the saints," he said, " you will see that all of them had a devotion to the Blessed Virgin; her intercession is most powerful, she is the Mother of God and the Mother of men."

If Brother André had lived today, he would likely have used a more inclusive language: "Mother of men, and of women, and of children too," so that no one would be left out!

The statue of the Blessed Virgin near the Oratory in 1909.

A Canadian peasant of the 19th century, Brother André did not move into high and abstract theology either about the Virgin Mary or even about Saint Joseph. His devotion to the parents of the Savior was very much in line with his family prayer.

Holy Cross Heritage

Marie Leonie Paradis, C.S.C.

His Congregation of Holy Cross also fostered the same devotion to Mary. The first superior of Holy Cross in the

United States had noticed how much people loved to visit the House of the Holy Family in Loretto, Italy. So he built a replica in the Holy Cross sisters' campus of St. Mary's, in South Bend, Indiana, and obtained from the Pope the same indulgences that were granted to the pilgrims in Italy. A well-known Holy Cross sister, Mother Mary Leonie Paradis, spent hours in this chapel of Loretto, applying her five senses to entering the intimacy of the Holy Family. She later founded the Little Sisters of the Holy Family and was beatified in Montreal, by Pope John Paul II, in 1984.

The *Santa Casa* of Loretto at St. Mary's, Indiana.

Brother André met her in 1875, when she first came to Notre Dame School, en route to St. Mary's, Indiana, where she led her first novices. Eight young women had arrived a month earlier, and used the brothers' community room as their convent. Leonie then was 35 years old; André was 30.

She entered Holy Cross when the sisters, brothers and priests still belonged to the one same community. The superiors hesitated before accepting her because she was frail, much like André; but the founder himself, Father Moreau, admitted her to religious profession when he visited St. Laurent in 1857. She spent the rest of her life collaborating especially with the brothers and priests.

Leonie knew André for 37 years, and saw him almost as many times as she visited her sisters at Notre Dame School. She founded a convent at the Oratory only a few months before she died in 1912.

Holy Family Chapel, built by Father Dujarié in Ruillé Heights.

Both André and Leonie shared the same Holy Cross heritage. Their devotion to the Holy Family was also shared by the priest who founded the Brothers of Saint Joseph in 1820, Father James Dujarie. The first chapel he built in 1811, for the Sisters of Providence he founded in Ruille-on-the-Loir, was also dedicated to the Holy Family.

Following the same heritage, André spent much time applying his five senses to entering and remaining in the intimacy of Jesus living in the company of Mary and Joseph. It was a typical and a most basic devotion of Holy Cross.

Connecting this with his great devotion to the Passion of Our Lord, he also invoked Our Lady of Sorrows, the special patroness of the Congregation of Holy Cross.

All this prayer, once again, was very simple. Let us read, for instance, a few lines out of one of his favorite meditation books, one filled with short and simple biblical phrases:

"Mary calls her children. Come, my children, come all to me. Am I not your Mother? Could a mother forget her children? Even if a mother would forget them, I will not forget you. If you could unite in one single heart the love of all mothers," it would be nothing as compared to my love for you! Then followed a prayer: "Oh Mary, how could I dare come near you? You are so pure, so holy, so perfect, so great! I am poor and miserable! Please enable me to join with all the angels and say, 'Hail Mary, full of grace....'" This is a very simple prayer, and it is filled with love.

Blessing of Mary's statue by Bishop Linneborn on August 22, 1909.

Brother André loved especially the image of Mary on the Miraculous Medal, the one with her hands open on each side. It was the one he had chosen to set on the grounds of Saint Joseph's Oratory in 1909. He wished he had one of these figures in his room, but he would not dare ask. One day, however, somebody gave one to him so he could keep it in his room.

He also prayed the Little Office of Our Lady, another of his favorite books.

In his mind, devotion to Mary and devotion to Saint Joseph were one and the same. As he repeated to his friends, "You cannot love one without loving the other. They belong together and you cannot separate one from the other."

His own charism in the Church was certainly to spread devotion to Saint Joseph. But he knew, for instance, that one of his remarkable friends, Sister Marie Anne LeBlanc, had a very great devotion to Mary. So he told her she should use a medal of the Blessed Virgin when praying with the sick. He respected her own prayer and never tried to impose his devotion to Saint Joseph on her. In fact, he himself used to put his medals of Saint Joseph before a statue of Mary for a moment of prayer, before he gave them to people.

In his own language of a 19th century Canadian peasant, he would add, "When the Virgin Mary and Saint Joseph intercede together, *that pushes hard!*"

Mary had a place of honor on Saint Joseph's property.

BROTHER ANDRÉ AS A NOVICE. Alfred Bessette became a novice on December 27, 1870; but one year later, the provincial council decided not to admit him to religious profession. The reason: his delicate health. Yet, he was permitted to stay as a novice, and finally made his first vows on August 22, 1872. His final profession took place on February 2, 1874.

His Many Friends

Brother André was a member of a community. He lived his entire life as a Brother of Holy Cross in a house of the community. His schedule, however, was different from the rest of the community. For 40 years as a doorkeeper, he often ate lunch and dinner before the others so as to be available to answer the door during the meals. In his last 20 years, he ate dinner five days a week outside the community, usually with the family of the one who drove him on his visitation of the sick. The superior himself prepared a list of those to be visited. So Brother André remained all his life, in the full sense of the word, a Brother of Holy Cross.

About the year 1900, however, his sense of a community took a broader meaning. He did not found a religious community but from the very beginning of Saint Joseph's Oratory, he was surrounded by a group of faithful friends who would never let him down. His friends supported him all the way. They lived under his influence, they always grew in numbers, and they certainly loved him.

Without them, his life would not have been the same. His friends were his faithful collaborators. They were the instruments who transmitted his inspiration, who took care of him when he was tired, who kept him in a good mood, who were the joy of his life. Whatever the situation, they were near. They were discreet, and yet always present. During all these years, people referred to them simply by saying: "He is a friend of Brother André."

Not very many saints had so many friends, not very many saints kept their friends for so many years. Maybe Saint Catherine of Siena would be another example, but the fact remains a somewhat special feature in the life of a saint.

For most of these friends, their relationship with him began in a similar manner — they were sick or in trouble. So they came to see him, and he led them to Saint Joseph. With all his simplicity, and through his radiant faith, Brother André knew how to create bonds that would last, bonds of a very real and heartfelt affection. He said, "We should be attached only to God." And he would explain to his friends that we should not show how much we love others. And yet everyone knew how much he loved them. And it would never have stayed this way for so many years, had he not shown the same unassuming respect and discretion towards them.

LOVE is our basic rule of Christian living. If Brother André had not LOVED people, he would never have put himself in the situations he chose, and people made no mistake about it. They understood that they were loved and he turned their affection towards Saint Joseph and to the Lord Jesus Christ. This was especially true with his most faithful friends.

Jules Aimé Maucotel

In 1905, a group of laymen joined him so as to foster development of the first chapel. These dedicated lay people were first gathered by one person who deserves a little more attention. His name was Jules Aimé Maucotel.

Deputy Registrar
Jules Aimé Maucotel.

It all began with an illness. During the fall of 1905, Maucotel suffered a sort of a burnout. His business went down, his creditors put pressure on him, he became neurasthenic. Then he heard about the doorkeeper of Notre Dame School and decided to go and see him. As soon as he met him, Maucotel became one of his most faithful friends. He made several novenas to Saint Joseph, came to Mount Royal and made the Stations of the Cross with Brother André every evening, then his life was changed. He went back to work, paid his debts; health and joy came back to his house and family.

No wonder this man devoted so much time, energy and good will to the early years of Saint Joseph's Oratory. His new Creditor was Saint Joseph, and he would do anything to please him. Maucotel played the organ, was the cantor and the sacristan, sold the candles, took up the collection, acted as usher; he was on the front line to get every permission in order to make the Oratory grow. Brother André called him simply his counselor.

When Maucotel took the initiative of taking Brother André on a trip to the already well-established Shrine of Saint Anne de Beaupré, near Quebec City, he had an idea in mind. As he walked out of the church, he pointed out the number of pilgrims to Brother André. "Some day," he said, "we are going to get even more people than that to the Oratory." "I don't believe it," Brother André answered, but there was a lot of joy in his eyes and in his smile when his friend looked at him.

Soon after that, Maucotel went to see the provincial superior, Father Dion, to talk about Brother André's project. But the latter was not impressed and told the enthusiastic layman that the whole thing could wait. It did wait for a couple of years.

Maucotel was 47 when he decided to bring Brother André's friends together. They held meetings, made plans, and collected 2,000 signatures. Finally, when they offered to take charge of the project, the provincial superior and the bishop agreed. In the summer of 1908, the chapel was enlarged with a 100-foot long shelter, it was heated, a sacristy and a steeple were added, and in 1914 the decision was made to build a large Shrine on the hilltop of Mount Royal.

This plan for the crypt-church was published on May 13, 1916.

Maucotel was by far the most active of Brother André's friends at the beginning of the Shrine, one who made his project possible. When the magazine was published in 1912, he collected subscriptions. An image of Saint Joseph was in every room of his house. At the age of 67, he had to undergo serious surgery. Brother André told him, "Do not fear; I need you," and everything went well.

He was 15 years younger than André and died one year after him in 1938.

Emile Gadbois

Another remarkable friend of Brother André was a university student who, about 1908, wanted to become a pharmacist. He went to the newly built Oratory one day to pray for success in his exams. It was on a feast day and many people were there. Brother André was talking and listening to the pilgrims. All of a sudden, during the Benediction of the Blessed Sacrament — about three o'clock in the afternoon — a young woman started shouting, "I am healed! I can walk!"

It caused a sensation, and the university student was particularly interested since he had had the opportunity to talk with Brother André just a moment before. "Do you have time to talk?" Brother André asked him. He certainly had. So they went

The chapel in 1908.

to sit and talked about the importance of a good Christian life.

From then on, Emile Gadbois never ceased to come back and climb the slopes of Mount Royal. When he finally became a pharmacist, he brought his customers to the Oratory. He owned a car then and became one of the most faithful drivers of Brother André as the latter visited the sick every evening after 5 o'clock, from Monday through Thursday.

Gadbois also had hardships. His wife caught tuberculosis and spent much time in sanatoriums. One day her lungs started to bleed and the doctors told him she would not survive the night. It was 3:30 in the morning when Gadbois came knocking on Brother André's window. "Come on in," said the old man. After listening to him, he said, "Let us make the Stations of the Cross. Your wife is doing very well." That was quite an act of faith to leave his wife and pray. But the two prayed the Stations of the Cross, in Brother André's own way. Then the man went back to his wife, only to find that she had in fact recovered. She lived five more years.

Gadbois later remarried, and his second wife was pregnant with her eighth child when she caught pneumonia. The doctor was quite concerned and consulted with two specialists. According to them, only one thing could be done: sacrifice the child, then at least the mother would be saved. Otherwise, both would die.

Gadbois then mentioned the name of Brother André, but the doctor said, "I am also a Catholic. I believe in my religion. Brother André cannot do a thing in this critical case."

Gadbois, however, did not give up. He went to seek advice from Brother André. The latter said, "It is not for us to sacrifice the life of anyone, even of a child. Why don't you let the will of God be done?" Gadbois and his wife agreed and, as a result, the life of both the child and the mother were saved.

Saint Joseph's Oratory in 1910.

There was also the case of his grandmother, who suffered from arthritis and could not bend her knees. "Bend your knee to the floor," Brother André said. "I can't possibly do it," the woman answered. "It is not a matter of knowing if you can," André answered. "Go ahead and do it!" She did and at that very moment, both her knees were healed.

Emile Gadbois was a very active man. When he was nearing 50, he suffered from angina which became more and more painful, but he could not stop working because of his family. He also kept driving Brother André to visit the sick in the evenings. For two years, he and Brother André prayed with confidence. They made novenas, they used the medal and the oil of Saint Joseph. But there was no progress, and the heart ailment became more and more painful. One day, however, as Brother André was asking Gadbois to drive him to visit the sick, he said to him, "Today I need not only your engine and your car; I'll take both your angina and your car!" From that time on, Gadbois was healed and never experienced any more chest pain.

Azarias Claude

Another friend of Brother André met him for the first time about 1907. He became the regular doorkeeper to Brother André's office and the one who drove him the most as he visited the sick in the evenings. He is also probably the man who was the most impressed and radically changed by Brother André.

Azarias Claude and Brother André on their way to visit the sick.

Azarias Claude was born to be successful. At first he was a butcher in a small village. Because of family problems, he had been living and working on his own since he was 14. In time he decided he could make a lot more money buying and selling cattle instead of slaughtering them, so he went to live in Montreal. He then became a furniture dealer and finally bought and sold real estate. He became a millionaire before he turned 40 in 1905.

Claude was a strong, tall man with steel blue eyes, and a kind of a cold look. But when you talked to him, he was as personable as any self-made, well-to-do, successful businessman. His wife was much the opposite. He was firm, she was gentle. She loved flowers and all the beautiful things in life; his purpose in life was to make money.

Through his business, Azarias Claude had to meet many people. So did his wife. As he himself put it with his cool sense of humor, "The women did all the talking about Brother André, and then the men repeated what they had heard!"

By the turn of the century, there was a lot of talking about the little brother from Cote-des-Neiges. There was no chapel yet, and brother was still the doorkeeper at Notre Dame School. That was when Claude's wife had a chance to talk to him. The stiff businessman could not believe it! "Women will believe anything! This brother is a charlatan, he's a quack! There are quacks everywhere and that one's no better than others. Why waste your time with such an old fool?"

But Mrs. Claude went back, time and again. And her husband kept asking every time, "How's it going up there?" And he too had heard another story about the "Old Fool of the Mountain." This went on for about eight years. Meanwhile the original chapel had been built.

One day Brother André asked Mrs. Claude, "Why doesn't your husband come?" She gave no answer then but the next time she went, she asked her husband, "I have to go and see Brother André. Wouldn't you drive me to the Oratory? Only drive me; you don't have to enter: it's just for a minute." Claude accepted. She stayed only five minutes, after which Brother André said to her husband: "Do come again, Mr. Claude. You don't have to be sick to ask for the protection of Saint Joseph." The man was amazed. He later confided: "I would have returned to see him that very evening, or the day after. But I was much too proud to do so, and I did not move for fear of what others might say. But I thought about him to the point of being distracted from my business. I wanted to see him again at any cost." He had been hooked.

Claude himself told the story many years later. "One week went by, and then I drove to Notre Dame School. 'Do you have time?' asked Brother André. 'Oh! I've got the whole afternoon free,' I answered. 'I'll be there in no time,' said Brother André. Then, he came back to me and said, 'Let's go up to the hilltop.' There was a bench in the shade and we sat there for well over an hour. 'It's nice out here,' said Brother André. 'We can talk, we are alone with Saint Joseph and the good God. Don't you think?'

"Then Brother André started talking about the beauty of the site. 'It seems to me,' he said, 'that one is closer to God on a hilltop. It took the superiors a lot of time and effort before they managed to purchase this beautiful piece of land.' Then he proceeded to talk about his projects for a shrine dedicated to Saint Joseph. And I congratulated him for it. But he said, 'Oh! It's not because of me. *Saint Joseph* wanted it. He is the *Great Owner,* along with the

Brother André in 1927, at the age of 82.

good God.' Brother André was talking to me about Saint Joseph as though he were a relative, or a member of my own family. I felt that he needed to talk, and that it did him some good."

Throughout this conversation, Claude had been very quiet. He did not talk much, not even about his own need for healing. Only during his third visit, did Brother André ask him, "What's the problem with your left arm?" In fact, his left hand was paralyzed. One day he had tried to free a group of people who were caught in a dangerous situation in an elevator, and his hand was crushed. "Would you like this hand to be like the other?" Brother André asked.

Claude said, "You know, Brother André, if the good God had some favors to do to me, there would be some more important matters than this for the salvation of my soul. My arm isn't sore and I can do my work. It's now been 15 years, so I'm getting used to it." Brother André looked at him and said, "Do you really mean this? Have you thought about it?" He said, "No, because I never had an opportunity to think about this."

"Well, in that case," Brother André said, "You will keep your arm the way it is. Later on there may be some more important matters. You may have to suffer. One should not forget that suffering is sometimes necessary." Then he proceeded to talk about the sufferings of Our Lord during his Passion, saying that unfortunately the world does not seem to understand that. They talked for a good while. Then he said, "Come often to Mount Royal, so as to entrust your difficulties to Saint Joseph."

They met and talked in this way about once a week for a few years. Then in 1912 Claude began going almost daily. The number of visitors to the chapel was increasing, and he felt that he could be of service in securing order in the waiting room, so as to let the people enter one by one.

Ten years later, Claude had gradually left his business and was full time in the service of Brother André. He was in the office an hour ahead of time, cleaning the place, welcoming the first visitors and talking to them before they spoke to Brother André. He would also talk to them afterwards, and tell them to wait if they felt he had not given them enough time. Claude also drove Brother André to visit the sick. Often they ate supper in his house, and when coming back to the chapel, they would pray — ten minutes, as they said — but it often lasted an hour.

Azarias Claude later said, "Brother André prayed as if he had been in the presence of someone from whom he was expecting an answer. And all this time, he was on his knees, without a kneeler, in front of a statue of Saint Joseph."

September 18, 1927.

"One hour is not a long time," Brother André said, "one hour to speak to the good God. We have so many things to ask of him, we could stay with him forever."

Claude's wife, who had acknowledged Brother André before him, had more than her share of suffering. She gave birth to 15 children, and they all died at birth. When she became pregnant a sixteenth time, Brother André said, "This one will live." The baby was a girl, and she is still alive today.

Some individuals are more aware than others of their spiritual journey. Claude was one of these. He was endowed with a vivid memory; he could remember whole conversations with Brother André, whereas most people remembered only some words or phrases which had been precious to them.

Thus even though Brother André never wrote a book, Claude remembered so many of his conversations with him that he put into writing much of his spiritual legacy, especially on the Christian sense of suffering.

"Brother André converted me," Mr. Claude wrote. "He led me towards a total change in my life. Before I knew him, my only concerns were those of a salesman, and making money was my purpose in life. He taught me how to renounce myself, how to do penance; I became a fervent friend of Saint Joseph and, from then on, I went to communion every day."

That was when Claude stopped trading cattle. "It had become an occasion of drinking too much alcohol," he explained later. So he started trading furniture instead, and spending more and more time at Saint Joseph's Oratory.

His attitude about his crippled hand, which he did not want healed, impressed Brother André. Here was an unselfish and a rare human being, who was ready to suffer the greatest sacrifices to follow Christ. "How are you doing," was a common question of the brother to his friend. "I'm well," was the common answer.

When Azarias Claude was 57 in 1922, he started to experience chest pain. It was diagnosed as angina. He then remembered Brother André's words, 15 years before, as they had talked for the first time about his crippled hand. "You are still young, maybe later you must be ready to suffer the greatest sacrifices.... One must always be ready to bear what suffering the Lord sends him." However, when he heard about the chest pain, André said to his friend, "Don't worry; you will not die of angina. You don't even have to fear a seizure outside of your house." Later, André said to him, "When you overcome this angina, you'll have to suffer from other illnesses."

Small consolation! Some time later, he had another seizure and fell unconscious for three days. His wife called Brother André. But the latter would not come. Instead, he acted like Jesus did when Lazarus was sick. "Your friend is very sick," she said. "Oh! Yes," was his only answer. As usual, Claude's wife remained discreet and did not insist. Two days went by.

On the third evening following her phone call, after visiting the sick, Brother André finally came to the house. It was supper time and Mrs. Claude was so worried she could hardly talk. But André was in a good mood. He talked and took time to eat before seeing about his friend in the room upstairs. It was on the feast of the Immaculate Conception, December 8, and Claude's wife considered this as a test of her faith. After the meal, Brother André asked to be left alone in the room with his unconscious friend. He knelt near the bed and prayed. Then he took Claude by the hand and said, "How are you doing?" The man opened his eyes, turned to him and said, "I'm well." And they talked together as usual. The wife could hear them and could hardly believe it.

When finally she climbed upstairs, she found her husband sitting on the side of the bed and talking. He said to her, "Bring my clothes, I want to get up." "It's too early," Brother André answered.

When he came back on the following evening, he asked, "How are you doing?" "I'm well," Claude answered, but his wife said, "He's caused me problems all day: he wanted to take his car and drive up to the Oratory." "Why didn't you let him go?" Brother André asked. "Tomorrow, he can come: he's not sick any more." Indeed, the following day was a full day of service for Claude at the Oratory. It ended as usual about 10 o'clock in the evening, after visiting the sick and praying in the chapel for some time.

But he had several angina seizures thereafter. Each time Brother André said, "Let's go and offer some prayers of thanksgiving in the small chapel, in order to thank the good

God." "Why?" Claude asked. "Did somebody ask you to pray for him." "No," Brother André said, "but didn't you have chest pains this morning?" "Well, yes I did feel some pain this morning." "That's the reason why we should offer prayers of thanksgiving to the Lord — because he is coming to you."

Brother André in his office in 1922.

Claude couldn't help saying, "Now, that's a funny way of praying. You thank the Lord for my chest pain?" "Don't you say that," Brother André answered. "You don't know what you're talking about." So they went to the chapel and Brother André prayed out loud with him for awhile.

Later, in conversations, Brother André explained, "When you suffer a lot, have you ever thought of the sufferings which Our Lord Jesus endured for us during his Passion? The time has now come to offer your share in his sufferings. Today, the Lord has heard your prayers and he is sending you something to suffer. God never forgets us. He knows your needs. Show that you are generous in accepting whatever he may send you in the future. Nothing will happen to you without him knowing it." Brother André talked then for more than an hour about the Passion of Our Lord.

Every time Claude had a new seizure, they went back to the chapel for some more prayers of thanksgiving. Brother André said, "If the people in the world knew how to pray better, if they understood better what our suffering is worth when it is well accepted, then it would help many of us come closer to God. We would be readier to accept our part of his sufferings.... The martyrs have suffered a lot, but their love was so strong that they were ready to suffer along with the Lord."

Azarias Claude was amazed: "But are we CALLED to become martyrs?" "We may as well be," answered Brother André. "If we live like them, we will... but the good God did not ask all of us to become martyrs. He has given us a much easier life. He only asks of us to be good Christians, to obey the commandments, especially the ones on the love of God and the love of our neighbor. But we must also be ready to suffer.... And one day, the good God will welcome us into his eternity forever, in the company of all those who wait for us there."

Claude remembered not only the conversations, but especially the look on Brother André's face as he was saying these things that seemed so natural to him. He was so much at ease with his friends, talking about the things of God as though he had been living every day with him. In much the

A statue from Oberammergau donated to the Oratory in 1925.

same way, he talked about Jesus, Mary and Joseph, as though he had lived all his life in their company. Talking about God and the saints was his whole life and the joy of his soul.

Claude remembered all these conversations with the founder of the Oratory in detail. As the latter said to him, "An hour-long conversation isn't really a long time. We have so many things to say, and it's so good to say them.... I may happen to repeat things I have already said. But what do you want? It's so good to talk about the things we love, and to say to the good God, 'I love you because you have loved us so much.'"

Brother André talked with Claude a little more about his early years than with others. "It's not necessary to have spent 15 or 20 years in schools and universities to love the Lord," he told him. "The most basic thing is how we have been raised. The soul of a child is formed at his mother's knee. Oftentimes, the children of a poor family are more generous and have a better chance to lead a good life. Those who have money must care for those in need, and it is not always true love to give them money. We can show how much we care by not judging others, and by visiting the sick who need comfort so as to understand that God is visiting them.... It would also do a lot of good to those in good health. They have a lot to learn from the sick."

"After talking with the sick," he added, "we should PRAY FOR THEM, so that they accept their share of sufferings for forgiveness of their sins. We can also pray to the Lord that the doors of heaven will be opened for them when they die."

"If indeed we loved the good God as we should, it would be a lot easier for us to put into practice the Christian virtues of patience and charity... for we can't love God without loving our neighbor. We would serve him better in our daily work. We would find it less tiring to say our morning and night prayers for those who are so busy that they cannot find the time even to go to Mass."

"God doesn't ask for the impossible, but he wants everyone to offer their good intentions, their day's work, and some prayers; that will help them a lot. The best Way of the Cross is when people accept willingly the crosses that are sent to them."

Claude used to say, "Brother André, you must be tired after talking so much to me." And Brother André would answer, "No, it does me a lot of good to speak with someone who understands me.... But you must be tired!" "Not at all...." And the two looked at their watches. "Well, do you realize that we've been talking for over an hour? Time flies when we talk about things we love."

Brother André was a delegate to the General Chapter of the Congregation of Holy Cross in August, 1920. It was held at the University of Notre Dame in South Bend, Indiana.

What they shared for hours was actually what they said to the sick when visiting them. For many people, sickness was an opportunity of thinking about their lives, which were not always successful. Sometimes, they doubted the goodness of the Lord. This was when a visit of Brother André was well appreciated. Usually, the sick were attentive to this kind of conversation, and all those in the house listened to him. Then he would tell the people to call for a priest in order to talk some more and to receive the sacraments.

Azarias Claude was prepared to act in the same way. He too talked to the sick, very simply, in caring for both their physical and spiritual health. And he invited those in the house to come and pray in the Oratory, using Brother André's words, "It's not necessary to be sick to come and pray. Saint Joseph and the good God are always ready to welcome you even though you're in good health." This phrase must have been repeated hundreds of times, and people listened to it. Many answered the invitation; they came and prayed in the Oratory.

Brother André was an educator, he taught people how to pray. "It's easy," he would say. "When you were young, you certainly learned how to pray at your mother's knee. God never gets tired of that, in fact, he's most pleased when you talk to him in the same way your mother did."

The old cattle dealer remembered all these teachings. One day Brother André had told him that a large fortune was a heavy burden when entering heaven. Claude — the self-made millionaire — gave enormously. One day some of his debtors came and saw Brother André, who in turn told his friend, "These are poor people, and they will never be able to repay you." Claude understood the situation and tore up papers that were worth at least $30,000.

Another time Saint Joseph himself seems to have come to the rescue as Claude could not solve a debtor's problem. A father of a family was about to lose the house he had mortgaged on a loan, and this time around Claude was not in a position to help. It was a matter of days. One evening, when Brother André was at Claude's house, a man rang the door bell, and left a thick envelope saying, "It is for Mr. So and So." They opened up the envelope and found exactly the amount of the debt. So they ran outside to discover who the man was; but it was winter and the falling snow had covered even the footprints. "It must have been Saint Joseph," they said.

Brother André with high-ranking Knights of Columbus.

Moses Robert

In Claude's wake we find another friend, Moses Robert. Here is his story, which happened in 1923 or 1924, precisely as he told it later:

"I was very ill with peritonitis. According to my physician, I was about to die sometime during the night. Then the landlord, Azarias Claude, drove Brother André to see me. I had been unconscious for three days.

"The first time I regained consciousness was when Brother André took my hand and shook it three times. He asked, 'How do you feel?' I answered with a groan. He squeezed my hand a second time and said, 'Something wrong?' I said, 'I feel terrible.' A third time he took my hand and shook it, and he said, 'Now it's going to be better.'

"At that moment I felt relieved as though a weight had been lifted from my brain, and down my body, and off my feet. I asked Brother André, 'Shall I be able to sleep?' He said, 'Yes, you will sleep, and tomorrow morning you'll come to the Oratory.' Then, I asked, 'Shall I be able to go to the Oratory?' He said, 'If you're not sick, then there will be nothing to prevent you from coming.'

"Then Brother André and Claude left my room. The nurse entered immediately and took my temperature, and it was normal. She called the doctor, who said, 'I'll be right there. Tell his wife to be prepared, because a drop in temperature is the sign that he's about to die.'

The plan of Saint Joseph's Oratory by Viau & Venne in 1926.

"My wife was pregnant. So the doctor came and took my temperature, which was still normal. I fell asleep while the doctor was there, and I was able to sleep all night until 9:30, on the next morning, when Claude woke me up and said, 'Get dressed, we are going to the Oratory.'

"I felt very well, so I got dressed, and the nurse didn't object to my going to the Oratory. Claude drove me to the foot of the hill, so that we might climb up on foot. I climbed without feeling tired, all the way up to Brother André's office. I said, 'Good morning, Brother.' He said, 'Good morning, Sir.' Then he added, 'Do you have a medal of Saint Joseph?' I said, 'I don't have any.' He said, 'Go to the souvenir shop and get one. Then go to the chapel and stop before the altar of Saint Joseph to thank him. Then, come back here.' Which I did.

"Brother André asked me, 'Do you have your medal?' I said, 'Yes.' Then I asked, 'May I eat, I'm hungry?' He said, 'Eat whatever you want. But do come again.' He rang his little bell so as to welcome the next visitor."

When Robert arrived home, the nurse did not want him to eat anything; but like a child, he cheated and ate three bowls of tomato soup while the nurse was taking some rest. She caught him in the act and called the physician, who said, "Well, if the man wants to die, let him go!" But in the evening, the doctor came again and saw that everything was going well. So he said, "I can only cure with medication, whereas Brother André can perform miracles!"

It was only then that Robert realized how things had gone so smoothly he had not even realized that this WAS a miracle!

Brother André enjoyed Napoleon Cantin's family life at Saint Joseph, near Lake Huron, in 1919 and 1922. Meanwhile, the children grew up.

He Loved People

Joseph Oliver Pichette

One of the most dependable witnesses during the trial for beatification was Oliver Pichette, who was 24 years old when he first came to see Brother André. He had been married only one year and he worked in a shoe store. But he was very ill. He had a stomach pain, an ailing throat, and a severe heart condition.

One day a certain lady came to the store, who suffered from skin cancer on her arm. She showed it to the salesman, who wanted to be polite and asked, "What did the doctor say?" "Well, I went to see a man," she answered, "who I was told is a saint. People climb up a hill and pray with him, and it seems that some of them were healed."

After some time, she returned to the shoe store, and she was radiant. She rolled up her sleeve to show her arm: the skin cancer had disappeared. "Brother André healed me!" she exclaimed.

Oliver Pichette was fascinated and later said to his wife, "We must find that Brother André."

On the following Sunday the couple climbed the hill to the Oratory, and waited in line with all the others to see him. He seemed to be very busy, however, and in fact something a little distracting was going on. A crippled man was there with his crutches. As he entered the brother's office, the latter said, "Give me your crutches and walk!" "I cannot," the crippled man answered. "I just can't walk without my crutches!" But Brother André insisted even more, "You don't need them, give them to me!" Finally, the man complied and he was healed.

Everybody was amazed, including the Pichettes, who had not yet been able to talk to André. Only at three o'clock, were they able to approach him and say, "Brother André, we want to talk to you." But he answered, "After the Benediction of the Blessed Sacrament." They waited. Then it was four o'clock, and then five o'clock. They wondered what was wrong with Brother André, who obviously was not interested in talking to them. "So you're sick?" he finally said, and went to do some other things. He hardly took the time to tell them to come back another day.

However they did come back — several times — especially on week days, hoping to finally talk to him. That was in 1911, and each day there was a crowd. So they waited, and they waited some more, and they kept coming back. The owner of the shoe store was aware of the situation of his employee, and he accepted it. But there seemed to be no way of talking to Brother André and things were getting worse.

After several months, they finally talked to Brother André, who told them what he used to say to everyone: to pray with confidence, to use some oil and the medal of Saint Joseph, and to make a novena. Twenty-four-year-old Oliver Pichette found it harder and harder to climb the slope with so little hope. After a year, he went to see a specialist from France, who explained to him everything about his illness. But things did not improve. While the doctor was putting

Oliver J. Pichette in his twenties.

some medication on his throat one day, Oliver suffered a hemorrhage. At this point Pichette spoke to the doctor about Brother André, with whom he had now prayed for a year without any result. The doctor burst out laughing, "You go and see that crazy old man?" Oliver answered by telling of the cures he had witnessed. But the doctor shook his head and smiled at him, "I just don't buy that stuff; I am a Mason. Anyhow, if you go and see him, never try to walk up the hill, because you could die any minute."

Oliver Pichette did not discuss the doctor's prognosis, but found it somewhat discouraging. "Listen, Brother André, I have been praying with you for a year. So many times you talked to me about a novena. Are we finally going to make one together?" "As you will," was always the brother's answer. But one day, he gave him the key to the small room above the sacristy of the original chapel. "If you want to," he said, "you may go up there and take some rest." This is where the novena was going to take place.

Pichette went to live for nine days in Brother André's room. All he needed to eat was a bowl of soup. Brother joined him every evening and prayed with him. By the time he had finished his long office hours and his evening visits to the sick, it was sometimes 10 o'clock, 11 o'clock, or even midnight. But Pichette could hardly sleep anyway.

Brother André used to welcome the sick into his room, which was above the sacristy, under the steeple of the original chapel.

For the first time he thought he was going to die, but he decided that this was a good place to do so. Let us read the rest of the story in the very words of the witness.

"I was with Brother André, and I felt O.K. with him. In fact I was more and more ready to go to God. Then, on the last day of the novena, I thought, 'Brother André is going to tell me now that the Lord doesn't want me healed, and that will be it.'

"That evening, Brother asked me his usual question, 'How are you doing?' I said, 'Listen, Brother André, you heal the sick; you should know!' Then he started rubbing my

chest with both hands. That went on and on, and I could see
him praying by the motion of his lips. Then he went to pray
in the chapel, downstairs, in the dark. After a half hour, I
went to join him. He was alone, motionless on his knees,
with his arms crossed. So I went back to bed. At two
o'clock, he came back to the room. There was another
young man sleeping in the other bed, with a pain in his leg.
So Brother André unrolled a small mattress and went to
sleep on the floor.

"At 4:30, his alarm-clock rang. His night was over. So
I got up and went to Mass with Brother André. Then we
came back to the room. The night before, Brother André had
put some veal and pork in a pot for slow cooking. He said,
"At 10 o'clock, you will add the potatoes." At noon, he
prepared some dough and, with a spoon, he added it to the
meat and potatoes. Then he added an onion, took a large
plate and filled it. He cut a thick slice of bread and gave it to
me. I said, 'Is this really for me?' He asked, 'Are you
scared?' 'No.' I said, 'I'm ready to eat it all.' And I did.
Then Brother André told me to go and take a walk on the
hill. I picked some raspberries, then I attended the prayer
service at three o'clock. I saw some people I knew, but I
was so happy I only felt like laughing. That evening, I told
Brother André I was going to PRAY FOR HIM.

"On the next morning, after the Mass, he told me I
could return home, because I was well. I had found the nine
days awfully long, but at that very moment, I would have
stayed with Brother André forever."

Oliver Pichette was healed. He took the trolley car to his
home near downtown Montreal. His wife had been spending

Brother André taking rest in San Pedro, Calif., in 1921.

the week with her uncle's family, 50 miles north of Montreal. On a hot summer day, Oliver Pichette rode his bicycle to the train station, took the train, and did the last five miles on his bike. "I felt stronger than I had ever felt before." His wife and everybody else were moved when they saw him in good health. He went to work in the field with the other men that very same day. No one wanted to believe it, and all said, "You are going to kill yourself!" But he was healed.

From that time on, Oliver Pichette, whose name was in fact Oliver Joseph Pichette, changed his name to Joseph, in thanksgiving.

He was 25 years old. From then on, he and his wife worked hard and became the owners of their own shoe store. They remained very close to Brother André and visited him often. Many times, when André needed rest, they took him to their home or their summer house for a week. In 1927, when Pichette turned 40, he had more time and, like Azarias Claude, decided to spend entire days welcoming the pilgrims into the waiting room. He also drove Brother André in his visits to the sick.

André noticed that Pichette was a discreet man with sound judgment, so he kept him as an adviser next to him in his office to deal with the people. Pichette also had a remarkable memory; and if many healings were not forgotten, it was due to him.

Dominique Cormier

Joseph Pichette brought several members of his family to Brother André, including his brother-in-law, Dominique Cormier. Cormier was already engaged to Pichette's younger sister, when he was sent to the First World War. Brother André told him to act as a good soldier and as a good Christian. He then turned to his fiancee and said, "He will return safe and sound." Then the soldier went off to war armed with a medal of Saint Joseph.

The original chapel stood in its place until the crypt-church was open to the public on December 16, 1917; then it was moved over to the right.

In 1917, he was sent to the front, in France. His fiancee kept coming to the Oratory to invoke Saint Joseph. Brother André comforted her, promising that her Dominique would come back. André had a keen appreciation of people and he had long understood that Dominique Cormier was a brave and dedicated fellow. Once he said to Miss Pichette, "Why don't you write him and ask him if he himself didn't ask to be sent to the front?" She found out after the war that André was right; he had guessed exactly what had happened.

Cormier then became another faithful friend of Brother André. He was at the Oratory every Sunday. He worked as a mechanic for an important automobile company in Montreal and had to travel a lot, but his schedule enabled him to serve as an usher in André's office, just like Azarias Claude and Joseph Pichette. He too was a regular driver of Brother André and welcomed him at times into his home for meals or some days of rest. Brother told him many times, "It is so nice to be here." The Cormiers' children loved him like their own grandfather.

Dominique Cormier was also a dependable driver. Oftentimes they drove long distances together. After a day's work, they would leave at 5:00 P.M., drive 130 miles to Ottawa, visit 10 or 12 sick people in the evening and then come back during the night. Cormier had a good, heavy car and Brother André said, with a broad smile, that he enjoyed traveling with a fast driver!

All these people wanted "souvenirs" from him. Azarias Claude bought him a black winter coat and he saved the old one as a relic, without mentioning it to anyone. Pichette had a shoe store and gave André new shoes; but kept the old ones as relics! Cormier gave a kettle to André and saved the old one as a relic. He said, "Brother André seemed to be so happy when boiling water in his new kettle!" They knew

that, humble as he was, he would never think they were collecting relics from him!

Dominique Cormier was one of the few friends of André who had not been healed. In 1936, when Brother was 90, Cormier finally suffered a mastoid infection that grew more and more serious. An operation was considered too risky, so his old friend said to him, "Saint Joseph will operate on you!" And in spite of his age, he started rubbing the back of Cormier's ears with oil, invoking Saint Joseph. Pichette was there as a witness and he remembered that André would stop to catch his breath, and then kept praying and rubbing the back of Cormier's ears. At one moment, he said, "Saint Joseph will heal him." Cormier, who was totally deaf because of the infection, heard him. So Brother André continued very smoothly, and Dominique Cormier was healed.

The doctors could not explain that; they had never seen anything similar. In spite of his old age, Brother André had wanted to leave a sign of his affection, and Saint Joseph had heard him once more.

Fire Chief Raoul Gauthier

One of the most interesting snapshots of André and his friends was taken with a group of Montreal fire-fighters on the feast of Saint Joseph on March 19, 1920. This may well be the case everywhere, but in Montreal, for every child, fire-fighters are the symbol of generosity and dedication — people who will do anything to save others. No wonder they associated so well with André, who was so keen about everyone in need; he and they really belonged together. Even today, Montreal firemen volunteer as ushers during the large gatherings in Saint Joseph's Oratory.

When the picture was taken, in March of 1920, Brother André was in the center of the group and Fire Chief Raoul Gauthier stood next to him. Here was another remarkable man who was a great friend of André.

Born in 1881, he earned his college education as a sailor. Then, at the age of 23, he entered the fire department and soon distinguished himself by his intelligence, even though he risked his own life in order to save others. Already in his first few years with the department he earned the Order of Merit for his remarkable services. He carried several people out of the flames and received a gold medal for his behavior as a perfect gentleman. He was courageous, unpretentious, caring, helpful, and most friendly to everybody. One phrase had become his trademark: "Keep smiling!" Articles were published about him in the papers during his early years of service, praising his quick mind, his practical sense, and his love of others.

He visited his colleagues in hospitals or in their homes when they were sick or injured. This is how he met Brother André. Once, he called him on the phone and said, "One of our firemen is in the hospital and he wants to see you. If you will, I'll come and take you in my car, tonight." Brother André answered, "Tonight, I can't go: it's Friday, and we pray the Stations of the Cross." "Well, then," said Raoul Gauthier, "may I go and pray the Stations of the Cross with you?" "Please do!" said Brother André.

From that time on, Raoul Gauthier went to the Oratory every Friday
night that he was free. Once he noticed that Brother André's voice was
not strong enough to conduct the
prayers, he volunteered to read with
another fireman, Oscar Marin, and
another friend of André, Justice Arthur Laramée of the Court of Montreal. From that time on, lay people
conducted the Holy Hour followed by
the Stations of the Cross Gauthier's

Chief Raoul Gauthier.

leadership in particular, was instrumental in making the
prayer service better known and in bringing several hundred
people to take part in the Friday night gatherings. Brother
André was happy because the Oratory had become once
again, in 1919, the work of fervent lay people.

Raoul Gauthier was elected Montreal's fire chief four
years later. When the decision was made, he was fighting a
blaze in downtown Montreal. They found him at work,
leading his men. His face was covered with water and
smoke, and a little blood from a scratch. He said, "You
wanted to see me?" "Yes," they said, "you've been elected
Montreal fire chief." "Thank you!" he said, and went back
helping his men.

Brother André found him a wonderful human being. He
went to his home and, there again, he became like a grandfather to the Gauthiers' six children. When he needed
some rest, their summer residence on the shore of the St.
Lawrence River was one of his favorite places. He enjoyed
their family life and became a close friend to them.

As fire chief, Gauthier did everything he could to modernize the equipment. Besides using his own imagination and creativity, he followed international conferences on fire fighting in the United States and abroad. He modernized the Technical School of the Montreal fire department. He also cared for the spiritual needs of his men, organizing conferences and retreats for them, in which he always participated. And from the time he met Brother André, he had a statue of Saint Joseph sitting on his desk.

This talented, wonderful human being died on June 17, 1932, at the age of 51. He had just presided over a ceremony in a cemetery, in honor of the fire-fighters who had died on duty, when an American oil tanker, the Cymbeline, exploded in the Montreal harbor. No one ever knew exactly

what happened but Fire Chief Gauthier and three of his men were killed.

Several days later, the bodies were still under water; and Brother André went to console his wife and six children in their home. The fire-fighters came then asking him to do something, so he went to the scene of the accident and prayed. He then took two medals of Saint Joseph out of his pocket and threw them into the water where the body of his friend had fallen. The other three bodies had already been found, as though the chief had once more wanted his men rescued before him. A few hours later, Raoul Gauthier's body re-surfaced, exactly where the two medals had fallen. Thousands of people attended his funeral as if for a national hero.

Gauthier had been a remarkable friend of André for 23 years. From then on, the whole fire department remained faithful to Brother André. Irish firemen called him: "The Saint," or as columnist Colonel George Ham had called him in his article of 1921: "The Miracle Man." "When you go to a fire," he said to them, "mind the fire, but make sure you have a medal of Saint Joseph in your pocket."

Leopold Lussier

One of Chief Gauthier's men, District Chief Leopold Lussier, became another friend of André in the early 1920's. André called him Leo, and Leo became one of his most dependable drivers. He was also a faithful witness in the trial for beatification, since he remembered a multitude of anecdotes about André, like the following ones.

Once the "Miracle Man" had become famous in the whole region, some people wanted to get all kinds of favors from him, even sunshine on a Sunday, that they might go out with their family! Some went as far as using blackmail in order to get what they wanted, for instance, "If we don't get what we're asking for, we will blow up the crypt during

Midnight Mass on Christmas eve!" That night, 35 fire-fighters were standing in the Oratory crypt-church and no one blew it up!

District Chief Lussier also noticed how Brother André welcomed influential members of other religions or denominations. Jews came to be healed. Freemasons came to him with large badges visible on their lapel. When his friends objected to his readiness in welcoming them, André answered, "Oh! That badge is only a small piece of tin! A human being is much more important than a badge, don't you think?"

Two women came from Lachine, on the far western side of Montreal; one was a Catholic, the other a Protestant. They ended up two of the most faithful participants in the Holy Hour and Stations of the Cross. Many Jews came

Labor Day, on September 6, 1925.

since they felt they were welcome. According to Leopold Lussier, André was even friendlier with non-Catholics.

He said Friday was one evening André always kept to himself. There was no way of getting him to visit the sick on that evening.

One Friday evening, André said to him, "You look so sad, tonight!" Lussier answered, "My daughter is very sick, at home. I wanted to stay with her but my wife said, 'It won't do any harm if you go and pray.' So, here I am." "Don't worry," Brother André said, "we shall pray for her." The district chief stayed and prayed, but he was most anxious to go back home. "Don't be afraid," Brother André repeated, "she is doing well."

After attending the Holy Hour and the Stations of the Cross, the man hurried home and his wife said to him, "Go and see your daughter." He went to her room and found her radiant, playing, and jumping up and down. Like in the Gospel, he and his wife realized that she had recovered exactly when Brother André had said, "She is doing well."

Leopold Lussier also had memories of people who were never healed. One had half of his face paralyzed. He came to see Brother André, who asked him to pray and rub his face with Saint Joseph's oil. He did it for a few weeks and, deciding that it made no sense, he gave up. "The poor man," said Brother André, "he may keep that for 15 years!" In fact, he was never healed; he died at the age of 43, exactly 15 years and one week later.

Picture taken by Colonel George H. Ham in the summer of 1921.

Like many of Brother André's friends, Lussier drove him in the evenings, after 5 o'clock, to visit the sick. They would then eat supper in his home with his family. But Brother André knew his friend had a lot to do since the City of Montreal was growing. He also had to be at home with his family.

Whenever there was a fire alarm, Leopold Lussier did not have to look very far to find his medal of Saint Joseph: it was always attached to his lapel!

The Two Marins

Oscar Marin, another fireman, also joined with Raoul Gauthier for the Holy Hours and the Stations of the Cross in the Oratory. Marin had a good voice and did the readings. He had a son, Oscar Jr., who also became a fireman and another regular driver of André. His family experienced numerous healings.

Marin's father had become almost blind and once broke his hip bone. Surgeons had decided that, due to his age, he would never walk. Brother André took him by the hand and said, "Come on, Daddy, don't be so lazy." He lifted him up to his feet and the man walked. The old man lived ten more years and he could walk till the end. Not long before his death, he was still with the others in Saint Joseph's Oratory.

A two-year-old grandson was also healed. Guy had pneumonia, and the doctor said there was little hope. Brother André came to the house and gently rubbed the chest of the little child, who started breathing normally and went to sleep. He was healed, and the doctor said later, "This man is a lot more capable than I am!"

A seven-year-old daughter was also healed of diphtheria, which was highly contagious and considered fatal at the time. Marin's wife was healed of an abscess. He was also present when a man who had a large spot on his face came to see Brother André and saw the spot disappear when he put some oil of Saint Joseph on it.

Marin was fascinated by the fact that Brother André spent so much time in prayer. He remembered that he spent hours in the crypt-church, perfectly still. He also remembered that when he drove Brother André in his car, the latter sat still and prayed his rosary. There was nothing to distract him, neither rain, nor storm, nor icy and slippery roads; he always prayed quietly, even in the worst of a thunder storm.

The building yard behind the crypt-church on July 30, 1926.

Antonio Valente

Italian immigrants had started to come to Canada in the beginning of the 19th century. But many of them arrived only after the first World War.

Antonio Valente was one of them. He drove his mother to the Oratory about 1920, to see Brother André, and soon became another close friend. One day Antonio was contagiously ill and about to be taken to a specialized hospital. Brother André came to the house, but did not enter Antonio's room. "Personally, I am not afraid of germs," he said, "but I wouldn't want to spread the disease. Anyway, you won't have to go to the hospital. No one will catch the disease in your home." In fact, Valente was healed, and no one else became sick.

Near Santa Fe, New Mexico, in 1921.

Valente's wife had a serious tumor and the doctors were quite concerned. Brother André said, "You won't need surgery." Valente then heard him say, in a lower voice, "Thank you, Saint Joseph! Thank you, Saint Joseph!"

Valente welcomed Brother André into his home several times, even for several days, when he needed rest. He also drove Brother André on his trips to New England, during the spring and fall. In 1927, he was with him in Bennington, Vermont.

In the early 1930's, Antonio Valente bought a movie camera, and produced the only movie pictures we have of André. Incidentally, when Brother André was beatified in Rome in 1982, Italian Television Network RAI broadcast these pictures; and the commentator said it was the first time ever that we had motion pictures of someone who had been declared Blessed.

Salvatore Marotta

Antonio Valente's sister was also cured. She had given birth to a still-born child and was very sick. Her husband, Salvatore Marotta went with Antonio to see Brother André, who promised that the wife would recover within two weeks. Out of gratitude, Salvatore Marotta volunteered as a regular driver for Brother André's visits to the sick.

Usually André would not allow a new driver to enter the home or the bedroom of a sick person, but once he became acquainted with Salvatore Marotta, he allowed him to pray with him and also to be a witness of the cures.

My Own Family

Before we end this chapter, I would like to talk about my own family experience.

When she was young, my mother used to live in Montreal, about a mile away from Saint Joseph's Oratory. She was born in 1906 and could remember the original chapel before the crypt was built, when she was only ten. During the winter, she and her friends would slide on sleds down the hill of the Oratory and they never missed an op-

portunity to talk to Brother André. He was nice to them as he had been with his young friends during 40 years as a doorkeeper in Notre Dame School.

Bernard LaFreniere, C.S.C., who wrote this book.

My aunt who is still alive also went to see him several times before her exams, when she was small. He welcomed her gently, told her always to pray with confidence, and assured her that she had nothing to fear with her exams.

An uncle of mine, my godfather, whose name was also André, became a friend of his, although he never drove him in his car. But during the 1920's, he attended the Holy Hour and the Stations of the Cross with Brother André's friends, who were about his age.

What struck my mother most about Brother André was his solid confidence in Saint Joseph. The only words she could quote from him were, "Have confidence. Why don't you have confidence?" That is very much in line with what Jesus said in the Gospel, that we should pray always and express our plea with the same hope and resilience as the importunate friend and the persistent widow.[1]

Once, when my mother entered the crypt-church to pray, Brother André was there in his usual pew, behind the statue of Saint Joseph, kneeling and perfectly still. She watched him for five minutes, 10 minutes, 15 minutes, and he did not move. So she thought to herself, "He must be dead." After waiting a little longer, she decided to go and ring the door bell of the residence. When Father Clement answered the door, she said, "I think Brother André's dead." He answered, "How can you tell?" She said, "Well, he's kneeling, and he doesn't move. He's been there for more than a half hour without moving."

Father Clement burst out laughing, "Don't worry, Jeanne; he's always like this when he prays."

Picture taken by Jack Doran near San Pedro, Calif., on Nov. 21, 1921.

---

(1) Importunate Friend: Luke 11:5-10; Persistent Widow: Luke 18:1-8.

Brother Andre's Death: His Public Recognition

The Last Days

In December of 1936, less than a month before he died, Brother André was 91 years old and still quite active in spite of his age. With his friend Azarias Claude he visited the sick on December 8, as he had done over the past 25 years or so. As usual, he ate supper with his driver's family. A picture was taken in the evening and ninety-one-year-old Brother André was in a good mood. But some time

In October, 1936.

before, the doctor had asked him to take some rest. Again he climbed into the car of one of his many friends and drove to Ottawa, where he stayed for a week with Mr. and Mrs. Philias Laurin, a family he knew well. Using the old road, Ottawa was 130 miles away from Montreal.

As was always the case, André's first concern was for the sick. There was a line-up at the door when he arrived, and he wanted to welcome them one by one even though he knew that, in doing so, still more people would come. In an interview published in the papers after his death, the Laurins told the reporter that, in spite of his age, in spite of the long ride, in spite also of his stomach ailment, Brother André welcomed them very gently. He was in a good mood. After a week, he went back to work in the Oratory.

André's grand niece was there, waiting for him. She was about to enter the Sisters of Mercy, whose motherhouse

Notre Dame School and vicinity in 1937.

was in Burlington, Vermont. Brother André talked to her about all the members of his family, whom he loved. Then he said to her, "If you choose to become a sister, make sure you'll be a good one!" She always remembered that.

December 24, he visited Antonio Valente.

Christmas Day, in 1936, was a Friday and, as usual on Fridays, Brother André did not go out. He stayed home and took time to meditate in front of the Christmas Crib, a scene he always loved.

On Saturday, he welcomed among his visitors a discouraged man whose life and fortune had been ruined by dishonest people. Brother André took time with him and explained that he should never be discouraged. "God will provide, my good friend. You'll never be in need for anything." The man was comforted. He regained hope and went back to work.

That Sunday, Brother André welcomed people at his office as he did every Sunday. One man was more insistent than others: his eight-month-old daughter was dying. Brother André said, "Let the will of God be done; you don't know what this child is going to be. If she comes back to health, it will only depend on Saint Joseph, not on me." But the man kept insisting and, in the evening, Brother André went with Joseph Pichette to see the baby, and the little girl survived: Saint Joseph had decided to heal her. André then

After the Great Depression the Oratory remained unchanged until 1937.

visited a friend of Pichette who was ill. Afterwards he went
to eat supper as usual, with the Pichette family, and then
went to visit another man, three miles north of the Oratory,
in St. Laurent, the Montreal suburb where the Congregation
of Holy Cross had settled in 1847.

Pichette later remembered that the pavement was slippery because of the falling snow. As they drove by the St.
Laurent hospital, the car slid a little towards it. And with his
usual sense of humor, Brother André said, "Don't enter the
hospital with your car — the poor sisters would be so
surprised!" Pichette answered, "Oh I'm sure, if we told them
ahead of time, they would open the doors even wider to
welcome YOU." The two men laughed heartily. Brother
André went on to say, "They are such good sisters and so
caring. And it is such a quiet place!" He had been there many
times to visit the sick; and after a moment he added, "It
would be a nice place to die."

At St. Laurent the man they had come to see was on his
feet. Brother André asked, as usual, "How do you feel?"
"I've felt just great," the man answered, "since 10:30 this
morning. This was what time it was when I called the
Oratory, and the superior told me you'd come and see me."
As usual Brother André sat down and talked for a while.

Pichette drove him back to the Oratory; then, as they
had done so many times, they went to pray in the crypt-
church, after which Pichette went home.

On Monday, the 28th, Brother André was sick with
what seemed to be the flu. He had a fever and the doctor told
him to stay home and not to go to his office. But during the
night between the 30th and the 31st, he rang his little bell.

The priest in the room next to him came to see what was wrong. André was trembling and very cold, and he said, "My right leg is like in the North Pole."

In the Hospital

On New Year's eve, the provincial superior, Father Alfred Charron; the Oratory superior, Father Albert Cousineau; and Doctor Lionel Lamy decided Brother André should be taken to the St. Laurent hospital, the only place where he could really have a good rest, without visitors. Only a few moments before André left for the hospital, the sisters took to his room one of the sisters who had broken her arm as she had slipped on the ice, so that he might comfort her.

He did not like the sisters to enter his room, but he spoke gently to her and told her she had nothing to fear.

The old section of the St. Laurent Hospital in 1937.

She was the last sick person he welcomed at the Oratory. Then one of his friends, Paul Corbeil, drove him to the hospital. They did it during the evening so that the news would not spread, as they did not want a line forming at his room in the hospital.

The next day, Father Cousineau went to see him. "Are you suffering?" he asked. "Yes, I am," answered Brother André. "But I thank the Lord for giving me this opportunity to suffer. I need it so much! Sickness is a good thing," he said, "for it helps us reconsider our past life and make up through repentance and suffering." Then

With his friend Paul Corbeil.

he leaned towards Father Cousineau and said, "Pray for my conversion." His superior almost smiled. They talked then about the Oratory. Father Cousineau had just written his superiors for permission to borrow a sum of money so as to finish the roof on top of the future basilica. "It's going to succeed," André said, "the basilica will be completed." He looked very happy as he repeated that a second time.

On Sunday, January 3, Brother André felt some pain in his right arm. He knew that the end was near and said, "The Great Almighty is coming." Only a few friends were allowed to enter his room, talk to him and pray the rosary with him as they had done so many times.

On Monday his right arm was entirely paralyzed. His good friend Paul Corbeil who had taken him to the hospital came to see him, but André could hardly talk. He was calm, but suffered and prayed in silence. In the world outside, his sickness made the front page headlines. Thousands of people were praying for Brother André.

During the night, however, he was lively and spoke more than usual to the sister at his bedside: "You don't know all the good that God is doing at the Oratory! God is so powerful." And he spoke about some of the most remarkable healings, especially those which involved a conversion. Then he said, "See the Power of God!... How good God is. How beautiful and powerful. He must indeed be beautiful, since the soul, which is but a ray of his beauty, is so beautiful."

Then he spoke about the Church in Spain, and about Pope Pius XI, who was also very ill. When the pain increased he said over and over, "My God. My God." He also repeated a prayer which he had learned many years earlier: "Oh Mary, my sweet Mother and Mother of my sweet Savior, protect me, help me!" Another one was, "How I suffer! My God. My God." And then came his last word: "HERE IS THE GRAIN...."

Was he talking about the mustard seed, the smallest of all seeds, that grows into a large plant? [1] Or was he talking about the grain of wheat that must die in order to bear much fruit? [2] Both are very much the story of his life and of his work on Mount Royal. It was four o'clock in the morning, when he lapsed into a coma.

---

(1) Matthew 13:31-31 ; Mark 4:30-32 ; Luke 13:18-19.
(2) John 12:24.

The next day, the doctors knew he would not recover. Since visitors would not tire him, his closest friends, his relatives, even the neighbors, were admitted into his room. All knew he was a saint and some wanted to have something touch him before he died, for a relic. During the following night, younger brothers and priests, some of whom are still alive today, were allowed to stay at his bedside. They were impressed as they prayed for the one who had taught so many people how to pray.

Later that evening, it became obvious the end was near. Father Cousineau came and stayed with the younger brothers and priests, who were supposed to take turns at his bedside, but finally decided to stay till the end. His breath became weaker and weaker; and finally at 12:50, on the morning of January 6, 1937, he passed away.

As it was the feast of the Epiphany, no paper was published that day, but the radio spread the news like the wind; and early that morning, all knew that the Holy Man who had founded Saint Joseph's Oratory had passed away.

St. Laurent Hospital on the morning of January 6, 1937.

His Heart Preserved; His Body Not Embalmed

Beside setting the date and time for the funeral, two rather unusual decisions were made early that morning. One was to preserve his heart; the other was not to embalm his body.

Preserving someone's heart is not very much a part of our North American culture. As I grew up a few minutes away from the Oratory, many of my friends found it weird. Why did Archbishop George Gauthier request that a heart be preserved?

Actually, he was following a European custom. In Italy and France, among other places, the hearts of famous people were preserved. In its biblical sense, the heart is the dwelling place of generosity, love, affection, commitment; all that is inspiring in someone's life. So the Italian and French preserved the hearts of their kings, their great army generals, the great benefactors of the nation. The archbishop decided there were even better reasons to preserve Brother André's heart, when people realized how much he had loved them.

Since then, the superiors of the Oratory have considered several times putting it back into the coffin where it belongs, but people did not agree. So it has stayed in the museum, under subdued light, and people stop there for a moment of meditation or silent prayer.

In March of 1973, it was stolen for some unknown reason, but after a year and a half, an anonymous phone call led the police to where it was. So today it is back in its place in the museum.

Brother André's tomb: "Poor, Obedient Servant of God."

Every day, people pray there as they do near his tomb, next to the crypt-church. Many actually speak to Brother André as though he were alive. In the mail, we find regularly phrases like: "I went to see Brother André and I said to him, 'Please, do something. I can't cope with this situation any more. Help me!'" People speak to him as they would to a dear friend living with God.

The other decision made early in the morning of January 6 was not to embalm Brother André's remains. Father Cousineau explained it later as a real act of faith.

They had decided that Brother André should lie in state for six days and nights, until the 12th, in an open coffin, in a warm church crowded with people. Now, Brother André had repeated so many times, in the wake of Father James Dujarié and of Father Basil Moreau: "God Will Provide."

"Deus Providebit." "We believe in Providence; Providence will see to it." Since this had been the way of thinking characteristic of Brother André all along, they decided that God would keep his body. The decision proved to be right — it was easily kept until the interment on the 12th of January.

Following the Hearse

On the morning of January 6, when Brother André had just died, a crowd gathered in front of the hospital. Altar boys at the parish, teachers and employees from Holy Cross schools, and many of his friends flocked to the door of the hospital. The sisters had no choice but to let them inside. Brother André was dead and all wanted to see him one last time. It lasted all morning and afternoon.

Friends of Brother André carried his coffin.

At 3:00, a black wooden casket had been purchased and his remains were brought back to the Oratory in a hearse.

A large crowd had gathered near the hospital, ready to follow in procession along the snowy streets, while church bells tolled his passing. A few hundred of the students of St. Laurent College, who were still on their Christmas recess, decided to go in spite of the rain and cold wind. The endless procession followed the hearse in silence, at a slow pace, between two rows of people who had gathered on either side of the street.

It took them one and a half hours to walk the three miles to Saint Joseph's Oratory.

When they entered the church, Father Cousineau asked young Brother Ubald Parr, who could sing and lead the crowd, "Do you have your office book?" "Yes, Father." "Take the Magnificat," he said. "We are going to sing the Magnificat." After the choir had sung a few Psalms, he addressed the crowd, expressing the feelings of all. He spoke briefly and then all sang the Magnificat, Mary's biblical song of humility and joy. Everyone was moved.

Lying in State

Outside, the drizzle had changed into a freezing rain blown by an increasingly strong, cold wind. But people kept coming from the 6th through the 12th of January, during the worst of a typical Canadian winter.

Two views of Saint Joseph's Oratory between January 6 and 12, 1937.

André's firemen friends served round the clock as ushers, and let people in, four by four, and out through another door after they had filed past the wooden coffin. One of Brother André's best friends, Arthur Ganz, decided to follow the crowd just like everyone else, and it took him four hours to walk from the bottom of the hill to the coffin of Brother André.

On January 7, the front page headline of a daily paper read, "One Million People Will File Past Brother André's Coffin." The journalist had observed that 110 people per minute walked in and out of the crypt-church of the Oratory. He multiplied this by the number of minutes in six days and nights and decided that one million people would come; and since the flow of people only increased, we now know that this figure was reached. On the morning of the 12th, the crowd was so large that it became

obvious that most would never make it inside the church. The firemen carried the coffin outside, so that all would have at least a final glimpse of his face from afar.

Nothing similar had ever been seen before. Indeed, Brother André had welcomed thousands of people in his office. But by visiting ten or 15 families every night for more than 25 years, he had entered most of the houses in the city. He had talked to everyone. He had entered the intimacy of their illnesses, their quarrels, their poverty and pain, their joys and sorrows. Now they realized how much he had loved them, and they would not go without at least paying a last visit, as to a dear and most personal friend. The cold winter only made their gratitude more obvious. No wind, nor freezing rain, nor snow, nor anything could keep them at home.

Special trains had to be scheduled from Canadian provinces as well as from New York and the six New England states, where he had visited people for two or three weeks every spring and fall. With the flow of visitors, Montreal's transit system was jammed and many more trolley cars had to be added to the main lines as well as to the one running in front of Saint Joseph's Oratory.

At least 30 newspapers in the United States published the news of Brother André's illness BEFORE his death. We don't know how many articles were published following his death, but the Oratory archives have saved 860 clippings

A picture from the 1986 feature film *BROTHER ANDRÉ*.

from papers, not only in Canada and the United States, but from all major cities like the *Figaro* in Paris and the *Times* in London. All the major news agencies sent a reporter to write about Montreal's little Brother André, and articles were published worldwide.

More recently, in 1986, the producer of a movie on Brother André found his best archive pictures in Hollywood. News reels were regular fare in movie theaters in 1937, and the movie makers had come and covered the event in order to make pictures available in all major cities.

Beatification

Church authorities had long realized Brother André was a candidate for canonization, and the first steps in view of his beatification were taken shortly after his death. His earth-

ly belongings were collected so as to be used eventually as relic.

A young priest who was at his bedside when he died, Father Henri Paul Bergeron agreed to write André's life story. He thus collected an important amount of first-hand information. His book, *The Wonder Man*, still sells over 100,000 copies every

Henri P. Bergeron, C.S.C. three years.

According to procedures, notices were posted at the entrance of churches, asking that any writing attributed to Brother André be turned over to Church authorities; they had to prove that his writings were in accord with the Christian faith. But Brother André almost never wrote anything and this enquiry did not last long. Only a few signatures by his own hand were found, along with two letters written to his family when he entered Holy Cross.

F. stands for *Frère,* which means Brother.

The longest part of the trial for beatification dealt with his way of life. Did he live in faith, hope and charity as a model for Christians? Did he practice and encourage justice, prudence, fortitude, temperance, and other virtues, as a model of Christian life? Was he faithful to his vows of poverty, chastity, and obedience as a Brother of Holy Cross? If so, then the Church would look for miracles, or signs from God, and eventually declare him blessed, and then a saint.

The purpose of calling witnesses to the bar, as before a court, is primarily to collect first-hand information so that the Servant of God may be better known to future generations.

Some 50 witnesses submitted to lengthy questioning in Montreal, in various parts of the Provinces of Quebec and

Ontario, and in Providence, Rhode Island, since he had spent three weeks there, twice a year, visiting with his family. These answers filled thousands of pages and were deposited in Rome in the summer of 1950. That was the most important part of the procedures. The purpose of everything which followed was only to double check on what the witnesses had said.

In Rome, a comparison of the testimony of each of the witnesses was made. Some additional information was sought. The Promoter of the Faith — also called the *Devil's Advocate* — wrote his objections and questions, and the lawyers for Brother André supplied the answers. Then on November 9, 1960, Pope John XXIII issued the decree introducing the cause in the court of Rome.

The whole study was then redone under the authority of the pope. Witnesses who were still alive were called to the bar a second time. New wit-nesses were summoned to an-swer some more specific ques-tions. That lasted two years, between 1962 and 1964.

The Church takes time in beatification procedures, and wisely so. A law of the Church even specifies that the final study on the virtues of a Servant of God cannot be undertaken be-fore 50 years have elapsed after his death. Blessed Brother André had a dispensation from that law because he was so widely known. His final study was done after 40 years, instead of 50.

The Devil's Advocate wrote his remarks and Brother André's lawyers supplied the answers. In the end, nine independent judges had to answer the last question, "Should Brother André be proposed as a model of Christian living?"

Their usual answer to this question may be either "yes" or "no". But when they say "yes", they usually like to point out the weakest point in their view, and if there is an agreement among them, some further research may be requested. It is a tradition followed by the judges. But in the case of Brother André, each one of the nine judges, without even knowing who the other eight were, answered, in Latin: *"Affirmative"*, which is a "yes", without finding any weak point. That is why people said Brother André made it *"Summa cum laude,"* that is "with the highest honors," or "with flying colors." We have every reason to be proud of Brother André.

Pope Paul VI recognized him officially as an outstanding model of Christian virtues on June 12, 1978. In doing so, he declared him worthy of the title "Venerable."

Less than four years later, on May 23, 1982, Pope John Paul II pre-

Pope John Paul II.

Brother André's beatification at the Vatican on May 23, 1982.

sided over his beatification in the presence of more than 30,000 pilgrims who had gathered in St. Peter's Square, at the Vatican. The feast of Blessed Brother André is now celebrated each year, on the 6th of January.

The organ in Saint Joseph's Basilica.

Epilogue

Let us conclude by quoting from a letter written in 1981, one year before Brother André was beatified. This cure was not officially acknowledged as a "miracle" by the Church. Therefore, it is called a case of healing, or a favor. It may not be so spectacular as many instant cures, but it remains a very good example of how people can pray with confidence and perseverance, no matter the circumstances, and how Brother André still supports their prayer.[1]

On November 5, 1965, a serious catastrophe hit the Delton family. John Anthony Delton and Larry S. went to Big Boy's on Capitol Drive, Milwaukee, Wisconsin, after working at Ewald's Service Station on Burleigh Street, at 11:30. They were returning from the stand, driving west on Capitol Drive, and they encountered two cars with two teenagers each, drag-racing. They all came to a stoplight. John, a seventeen-year-old senior in high school, tried to get way over to the curb in the right lane. The grey Chevrolet on his left side side-swiped John's black Fury, and John lost control. The car swung around and slammed into a tree, hitting the door on the driver's side.

Since he was not wearing a seat belt, the impact pushed John to the right. His friend was not injured but the wheel

---

(1) We are grateful to Mrs. Phyllis E. Delton, who allowed us to publish the case of her son as she reported it in 1981. She wrote: "Why should we hide all the facts and circumstances of John's recovery? We feel the whole world should know."

pinned John's left side, punctured his lung, filled the trachea with blood, thereby shutting off oxygen to the brain. His lung collapsed and he had air in his chest cavity. Likewise, he received internal injuries to his stomach and kidneys.

He had to be pried loose with crowbars to be removed from under the wheel, and was rushed to County General Hospital at 12:15 on November 6.

The chaplain gave him the Last Sacraments, although he was unconscious. Not a muscle moved.

The doctors glanced at him and pronounced him dead. But one doctor thought he would chance it. After receiving the necessary signature at 1:20, he performed tracheotomy and the blood gushed forward. The time between the accident and the tracheotomy was too long to avoid brain damage. The doctor said that John was black and blue, stiff and lifeless, but when the tube was placed into the trachea, he showed signs of life. John's left lung had also collapsed. Five doctors were present.

John was in the operating room from 5:00 until his parents saw him at 10:00. He looked terrible, had lacerations to the left arm between the elbow and the wrist. He also had tubes in his stomach, left lung, and kidneys. He was not expected to live and the doctor said that persons with much less damage did not make it.

Sunday, November 7, there was no change. On the next day, he caught pneumonia in both lungs.

Tuesday, he became worse and received Extreme Unction again. He was placed under a "thermos" blanket to keep his temperature down, as it rose to 106 degrees.

Brother André a few days before his 84th birthday, on August 9, 1929.

Wednesday: John was worse and the doctors called the family notifying them that they should expect him to die. So Frank and Phyllis, his father and mother, began to make funeral arrangements.

At that point *there was no hope,* but Phyllis Delton and her friend Marie S. remembered a trip they had made to Montreal, to Saint Joseph's Oratory in 1964. When they saw John's condition getting worse they said, "Let us ask

Brother André for help." They took a medal of Saint Joseph, some oil, and anointed John's hands, and feet, and head, with the Sign of the Cross and they prayed. John's mother promised that if it was God's Holy Will that he live with no brain damage, they would make a pilgrimage to Montreal and attend Mass on three consecutive days in thanksgiving.

Marcel Lalonde, C.S.C., Oratory Rector, 1962 to 1992.

Again on Friday, John was bleeding from his lungs, stomach, and kidneys. His mother came at 6:00 every morning. John was given blood transfusions and had a stress ulcer.

On the following week, he showed no improvement, but he was not getting worse. All his parents could do was to appeal to God and ask everybody for prayers. Ten days after the accident, the Deltons received a letter from Saint Joseph's Oratory in Montreal, Canada, where the Fathers wrote that they would make a novena to Saint Joseph and Brother André for John.

On the following Thursday, November 18 — two weeks after the accident — the doctors said that a miracle had happened, as there was no trace of an ulcer when X-rays were taken." The family prayed with even more confidence.

On Thursday, John had his eyes open from 10:20 till 12:00 noon. In the afternoon, the doctor said that they would inject a fluid into the blood vessels so they could X-ray the brain to see if they could alleviate whatever was there. The "angiogram" was taken on the next day and doctors explained to John's parents that unconsciousness had really been caused by a lack of oxygen.

Nevertheless, at the beginning of the following week, John's mother kept praying, and even did some exercises with him. The therapist showed her how. She said, "It seemed that I was able to relate to John. He began to answer me by blinking his eyelids twice for yes."

On November 21, John was moved from the intensive care unit. His parents realized that he was paralyzed on the whole right side, arm and leg.

Thursday, November 25 was Thanksgiving Day. The Deltons went to see John in the afternoon, but all he could do was to look at them without saying a word.

Janie, his sister, and his mother went to see him in the morning and found him sitting, strapped in a chair. His head just fell anywhere, and he looked terrible.

Saturday, three weeks after the accident, John began squeezing his mother's hand with his left hand for "yes." She was able to give him a drink, and he did so well that she asked the doctor if John could have a soup as he was getting thin.

Saint Joseph's Oratory basilica was completed in 1966.

On December 5, one month after the accident, John learned how to use a straw. He also learned to nod his head for "yes" and to shake his head for "no." In the following days he learned a few words.

Six weeks after the accident, John was moved to Unit II of the General Hospital. His parents found it very depressing as the nurses called John a "nincompoop" and accused him of being stubborn. When he was in intensive care his temperature had risen over 106 degrees; the doctors were convinced that for sure John would have brain damage. His mother brought him some food on December 16, but his temperature began to rise again to 99.2. It was obvious that he could make no effort.

On January 18 — one and a half months after the accident — John came home from the hospital. His family had to arrange the furniture so he could hobble from his bedroom to the bathroom. No one could tell how much he would recover.

John had a physical examination on January 24, and the report was: "The patient has improved remarkably, has no evidence of language disturbance." During the following six months, therefore, he received physical, occupational, and speech therapy.

In September, 1966, less than a year after the accident, he went back to high school and graduated in June, 1967. He continued his studies and in December, 1972, graduated from Oshkosh University with the degree: Bachelor of Science in Education.

On June 6, 1981, when the case was reported to Saint Joseph's Oratory, John was a youth counselor in a school. A more recent letter from his mother indicated that, in 1989-1990, he was still serving in the same capacity, in the same school, and that this was his tenth year.

Pope John Paul II praying at Blessed Brother André's tomb
on September 11, 1984.

A Faith Stance

This story echoes hundreds of letters we receive at the Oratory every year, and the many events that happened in Brother André's time.

Some healings may be more spectacular, especially when they take place instantly at Brother André's tomb. Some were and some will be officially recognized by the Church, according to well established criteria. But we must remember that any clear evidence of a "miracle" will never PROVE the existence of "miracles," because they are "signs," not "proofs" of the Living God.

Indeed no one has ever proved the existence of God in such a way as to be convincing to everyone; on the other hand, no atheistic regime, however strong, has successfully proved his non-existence.

Faith is a free gift and a free choice, much as love is. The signs given by God can only be seen through the eyes of faith, just as any sign of affection or love is recognized only by someone who loves.

God's love endures forever; his signs were given to every generation. Whatever the needs or the circumstances, whatever the failures, the medical evidence, or the time it may take, believers everywhere pray, hope and act with confidence, and in the end their prayer is heard.

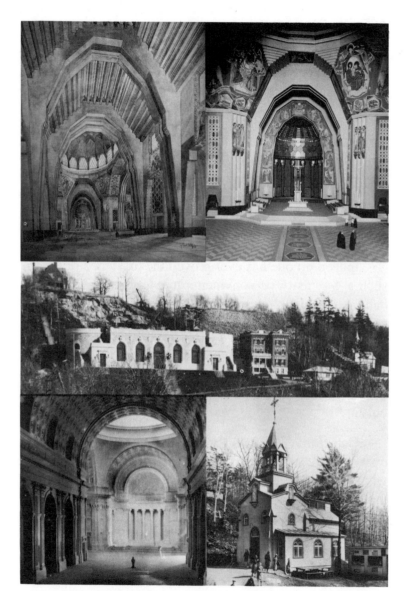

The plans of architects Viau & Venne (above) in 1926, Dom Paul
Bellot in 1937, and Gilbert Moreau in 1954 (top). Two views of 1924.

Saint Joseph's Oratory today.

Index

*Asterisks refer to pictures.